Kings and Carpenters

One Hundred Bible Land Jobs You Might Have Praised or Panned

by Laurie Coulter
art by Martha Newbigging

annick press
toronto + new york + vancouver

We acknowledge the support of the Canada Council for the Arts, the Ontario Arts Council, and the Government of Canada through the Book Publishing Industry Development Program (BPIDP) for our publishing activities.

ONTARIO ARTS COUNCIL
CONSEIL DES ARTS DE L'ONTARIO

Cataloging in Publication

Coulter, Laurie, 1951 -
        Kings and carpenters : one hundred Bible land jobs you might have praised or panned / by Laurie Coulter ; art by Martha Newbigging.

(Jobs in history series)
Includes bibliographical references and index.
ISBN 978-1-55451-227-0 (bound).—ISBN 978-1-55451-226-3 (pbk.)

        1. Occupations—Israel—History—Juvenile literature. 2. Occupations—Palestine—History—Juvenile literature. 3. Iron age—Israel—Juvenile literature.
4. Iron age—Palestine—Juvenile literature. 5. Canaanites—Juvenile literature.
I. Newbigging, Martha II. Title III. Series: Jobs in history series.

HD8660.C69 2010   j331.70093309'014   C2009-904944-9

Distributed in Canada by:
Firefly Books Ltd.
66 Leek Crescent
Richmond Hill, ON
L4B 1H1

Published in the U.S.A. by Annick Press (U.S.) Ltd.
Distributed in the U.S.A. by:
Firefly Books (U.S.) Inc.
P.O. Box 1338
Ellicott Station
Buffalo, NY 14205

Printed in China.

Visit us at: www.annickpress.com
Visit Laurie Coulter at: www.lauriecoulter.net
Visit Martha Newbigging at: www.marthanewbigging.com

To Lindsey
— L.C.

To my brother, Joey
— M.N.

CONTENTS

INTRODUCTION

A black iron fry pan sits on the stove. It looks dull, solid, and not much fun — no buttons to push, no blades to whir, no timers to *beep, beep, beep*. How interesting could six centuries named after iron possibly be? Actually, the people who lived during the Iron Age, which ran from 1200 to 586 BCE (Before the Common Era, or year 1), could probably have done with a little less excitement and a lot more boredom. This was particularly true for those who made their living at the eastern end of the Mediterranean Sea on a bridge. A land bridge, that is.

Living on a section of land squeezed between the sea, mountains, and desert would have been fine for the inhabitants, the Canaanites, if the bridge hadn't also linked three continents: Europe, Asia, and Africa. People from other places used this small piece of land (about the size of Lake Michigan) as a highway for trading goods and moving about. In the process, the bridge dwellers picked up new ideas and new ways of doing things.

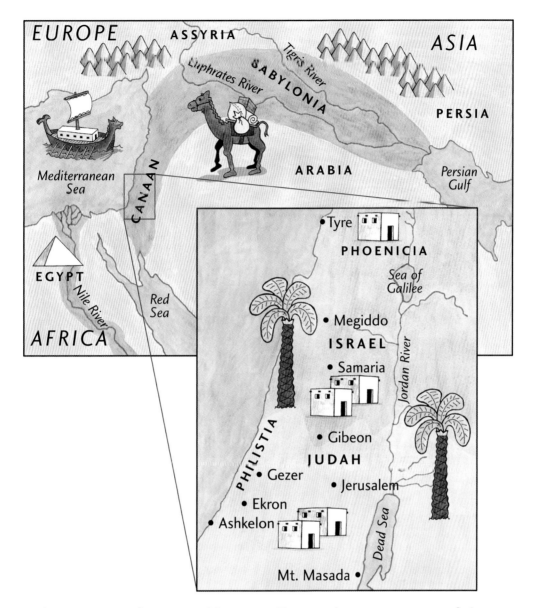

That was an advantage. However, Egypt, the superpower of the time, wanted to control Canaan because of its central location and the food and goods its people produced. To keep the peace, the Canaanite kings paid tribute — the best stuff their city-states grew or made — to the Egyptian pharaohs. Many years passed like this, until one year it stopped raining.

In the ancient Mediterranean world, the subtropical climate made farming a challenge at the best of times. A winter rainy season followed a summer dry season. But for several

generations, beginning around 1200, very little rain fell in the region. The severe drought caused widespread famine, forcing people to leave their homes in search of better land and times. Some groups of people ended up in Canaan, including the Israelites, who arrived from Egypt, and the Philistines, who came by ship, possibly from the Aegean Sea area. By the end of the Iron Age, the Canaanites had adopted the Israelite way of life, except along the northern coast, where they became known as Phoenicians. Everyone fought with one another and then traded goods in times of peace. They took turns being bossed around by Egypt, then Assyria, and finally Babylonia.

Today, men and women athletes run, bike, and swim in Ironman triathlons throughout the world. They must be exceptionally strong in body and mind to take part in these grueling long-distance races, often held in wilderness locations. But what if you had to be that tough and determined in your normal life? The people who lived in the part of the world that is now Israel, the Palestinian territories, and parts of Jordan, Lebanon, and Syria were Iron Men and Women every day. Most worked many hours a week at physical labor. They often walked long distances, sometimes across deserts. Some climbed towering date palms barefoot; others sailed out into the Mediterranean with no navigational tools to guide them. They fought off enemies with simple slings and arrows,

never knew when they might meet unfriendly bears or lions in their travels, and nurtured crops on hillsides with barely enough water to grow a chickpea, let alone fruit trees and grapevines. In addition to working very hard, they coped with the fear and heartbreak of war, earthquakes, drought, and disease.

Despite such challenges, the Israelites, the Phoenicians, and

the Philistines set down deep roots on the little bridge of land they shared. They faced the future with hope by working together in their family groups, developing a strong religious faith, and nourishing their spirits with music, crafts, gardens, and stories.

THE WRITTEN WORD

Ancient Canaan is often referred to as the Bible Lands, because the Hebrew Bible, also known as the Old Testament, talks about the people who lived there during the Iron Age. The Bible's many different authors wrote down ancestral stories and songs from the Israelites' distant past as a document of faith. However, the Bible also opens a fascinating window into the thoughts and times of the Israelites and their neighbors.

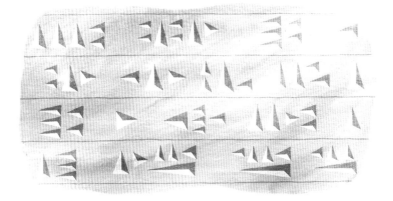

Cuneiform writing

Without a writing system, the Bible could not have been passed down to us at all. Cuneiform writing from Mesopotamia dates to 3100 BCE, followed by Egyptian hieroglyphs not long afterwards. The first method used dozens and dozens of skinny triangles to stand for syllables or words, and the second used pictures to do the same. Much later the Canaanites invented an alphabet in which each symbol stood for one sound. That led to the Phoenician alphabet (invented about 1100 BCE), which spread to Israel and eventually throughout the world, becoming the ancestor of all Western alphabets.

Egyptian
hieroglyphs

Cn u rd ths? Of course you can, particularly if you know how to text message. The Phoenicians not only cut down on the number of symbols needed for writing, they cut out the vowels altogether. Reading and writing became much, much easier. Still, most people — farmers, for example — didn't need to know how to read to do their jobs. Those who did — kings, scribes, clerks, governors, and other royal workers — probably taught their children to read and write at home; archeologists have uncovered no schools from this era, although that doesn't prove they didn't exist.

Letters from the Phoenician alphabet

Writing from the ancient past continues to be discovered today. Not long ago, archeologists found pieces of a locally made clay storage jar in the ruins of a Philistine town at Ashkelon, Israel. A scribe had written on one of the fragments sometime before the tenth century BCE. No one can read what he wrote, but researchers believe that it can be traced to writing systems used in the Greek islands. This discovery is the first sign that the Philistines were a literate people when they arrived on the coast of ancient Canaan, possibly from those same islands. If more examples of their writing can be found, experts might be able to decipher what the long-ago scribe wrote.

HOT DIGS

Beginning in the mid-1800s, the Bible Lands became a popular region for archeological "digs." Some people were eager to discover the whereabouts of the cities, towns, palaces, and temples mentioned in the Bible. Others were more interested in hunting for treasure — gold and jewels buried in tombs. Even today Israel is one of the most excavated countries in the world, with hundreds of digs carried out each year. (That's why the ancient Israelites dominate this book; more is known about them than about their neighbors.)

TELL ALL, SIR FLINDERS

Small hills or "tells" (from the Hebrew word *tels*) dot the landscape of the Bible Lands. A tell is formed when people tear down a mud-brick building and build a new house over the debris of the old one. Over many generations, a mound rises on the spot. In 1890 British archeologist Sir Flinders Petrie was the first person to figure out that these human-made hills held a secret history.

By digging down through the Tell el-Hesi south of Jerusalem, Petrie exposed each layer of settlement and its time capsule of pottery fragments and metal or stone tools. He noticed that the styles of jars and pots changed from layer to layer and suggested that broken pottery held the clue to dating archeological finds. Other nineteenth-century archeologists didn't think much of his idea, but today his dating system is widely used. Here's how pottery chronology works: Broken pottery that is unearthed with coins or royal seals can be dated. When archeologists discover a similar style of pottery at another site, they can compare the two and put an approximate date on the second find.

Despite all this work, many questions still cannot be answered about the Iron Age people from this part of the world. Were the children whose remains were found buried in large jars sacrificed as part of a religious ritual? Do the stone foundations of buildings at Megiddo in Israel indicate that they were food storehouses or government stables? Why did people bury more than 1,000 dogs in a cemetery in the port city of Ashkelon? Solving such mysteries is what makes archeology so exciting.

Modern archeologists continue to dig for answers. Sometimes more than 100,000 pottery fragments are studied from just one excavation alone. However, these days archeologists are interested in much more than pottery, bones, and the remains of ancient buildings. Plants, underwater shipwrecks, even excrement can provide clues to ancient people and the work they did:

• The tiny remains of ancient seeds and pollen reveal what crops people grew.

• Even tinier plant crystals called *phytoliths*, which are found in the bottom of cooking pots and storage jars, can help answer questions about food storage and preparation.

• Ancient shipwrecks reveal how ships were built, where they traveled, and what kinds of cargo they carried.

• *Coprolites* is a fancy name for fossilized poop. Archeologists are always happy to find a dump at a dig. Excrement can reveal what people ate and the types of parasites that lived in their intestines.

PEOPLE ON THE MOVE

At the beginning of the Iron Age, the Israelites built farming villages in the highlands in the middle part of Canaan. About 25 years later, the Philistines landed on the southern coast, conquering several Canaanite cities. Shortly afterwards, Egypt lost control over the Bible Lands, leaving no superpower in charge. Free from foreign empires, the Phoenician city-states to the north entered a golden age of maritime trade. Much zipping about on the Mediterranean.

Eventually, the Israelites set up a state ruled by a king. They began building new cities, with the largest numbering about 5,000 people. Unlike the dozen or so Phoenician and Philistine rulers, who each led a separate city-state, the Israelite monarch ruled over a nation-state of villages, towns, and cities. The population of what today is Israel and the Palestinian territories reached about 400,000.

The Philistines began expanding outwards from their city-states on the coast, clashing with the Israelites. Much pushing and shoving.

1200–1000 BCE

1000–800

More pushing and shoving. The Philistines faded as a major political or military force after they were defeated in battle by David, the Israelite king, about 990. Six decades later, the Israelite kingdom split into two: Judah, with its royal city of Jerusalem, to the south, and Israel, with its capital of Samaria, to the north.

The Phoenicians set up trading colonies around the Mediterranean, including the famous port of Carthage in North Africa.

Major pushing and shoving. Assyria, a Mesopotamian kingdom located in today's northern Iraq and southeastern Turkey, began to expand west. A mighty military power, Assyria was determined to control the Bible Lands' profitable trade links. In 876, its armies reached the Phoenician city-states and may have demanded tribute in the form of precious metals and luxury goods. In 734, Assyria defeated first the Philistines, then both Israel and Judah, destroying cities that refused to pay tribute.

800–700

700–586

More major pushing and shoving. Babylonia, in modern times southern Iraq, eventually took over from Assyria as the superpower controlling the Bible Lands. When it demanded tribute, two of the Phoenician cities and Judah revolted. During years of war, many of the region's inhabitants were deported to Babylonia.

The Philistine culture ended with the destruction of its cities at the end of the sixth century. Jerusalem was destroyed in 586, marking the end of the kingdoms of Israel and Judah. The Phoenician cities survived, but barely. When Cyrus II of Persia defeated the Babylonians, he allowed the exiles to return home in 538 BCE.

SURVIVING TOUGH TIMES

The old saying "When the going gets tough, the tough get going" could have been written about the Israelites and their Iron Age neighbors. So how *did* they "get going" in tough times? For the most part, they tackled their problems by standing together and helping each other out.

All ancient societies were based on the family, and the peoples of the Bible Lands were no different. To put food on the table and a roof over their heads, not to mention protect themselves from wild animals and human invaders, households worked together in family groups of grandparents, parents, aunts, uncles, sons and daughters, and cousins. The elders of the family passed down their knowledge to the younger generation and kept the history of their ancestors alive in stories told at the evening meal. Very large families were called clans or tribes. As time went on, some clan chiefs became kings, ruling over tribal kingdoms from cities. Most people lived in farming villages within walking distance of the fields, orchards, or olive groves. They grew different types of cereals and vegetables, in case one crop failed. They also raised sheep and goats for their meat, wool, and milk. Some farmers worked part-time as craftspeople, while metalsmiths and other artisans made a full-time living producing tools, ornaments, and weapons.

All of these so-called "ordinary people" paid taxes to keep the upper-class city folk — the king, his family, the royal staff, the high priests, and the military generals — fed, clothed, and housed.

Wealthy nobles, large landowners, and prosperous traders probably popped in and out of the royal court as well, tossing their capes to a lowly servant or slave as they swept into the palace on court business.

The ancient Israelites described their main cities and the towns and villages that surrounded them as "mother and daughters." The mother of all cities was the royal city with its palaces, public buildings, markets, and major religious shrine or temple. Regional cities held military headquarters, businesses, storage buildings, smaller shrines, and a market. Some people in little cities continued to farm, while the big cities filled with officials, crafts-people, priests, shopkeepers, and top soldiers. During times of war, the mother city helped defend the people of the daughters.

As for real sons and daughters, children learned and worked alongside their parents — boys mainly as farmers and girls as homemakers. They worked hard, but, just like children today, they looked forward to religious celebrations and the treats, dancing, and singing that made these days special. When they weren't helping their parents, children played with toys — clay or wood model wagons, tiny dishes, and dolls. They tossed cloth balls, twirled tops, and made funny buzzing sounds with bull-roarers, small disks attached to pieces of string. Hide-and-seek and board games were popular, too. Unlike you, though, boys and girls had little choice in the work they would do as adults. Most Iron Age children followed in their parents' footsteps. Think you're tough enough to live in the Iron Age?

To find out, turn the page!

CHAPTER 1

FARMING VILLAGE JOBS

Growing crops and raising livestock has always been tricky. This was particularly true in the Bible Lands, where water was scarce, tools were primitive, and plant and animal diseases had no cure.

Here's what not to do if you're a peasant farmer in biblical times:

• *Be a loner.* Living close together and sharing chores with family members saved farmers and their wives time and energy. Men farmed the land belonging to their clan (extended family) or rented land from a large landowner. Women worked in white-plastered houses, jammed together in villages near a spring or a well.

• *Ignore your elders.* Parents taught their children the skills they needed to survive on their particular plot of land. If you decide not to learn about the local soil types, the best crops to grow in the area, and neighborhood weather patterns, kiss your career in agriculture goodbye.

• *Gobble up any extra crops you raise.* Well, that's just dumb. The very practical Iron Agers knew enough to save or trade any extras. They traveled between villages on foot, using donkeys to carry extra food, wine, or oil that their village had produced and that they hoped to trade with other villages for something they needed.

Village Elder

An ad for this job might read as follows:
WANTED: GRANDFATHERS WHO ARE EXPERT FARMERS AND WISE PROBLEM SOLVERS.

In your Israelite village of about 180 people, no one elects, hires, or even pays you to do this job. After your own father dies, you take his place as head of the family and village elder. Your most important task is to teach the next generation how to grow enough crops and raise enough animals to survive on your family's plot of land. Sadly, you don't have much time to do this. In the biblical era, you probably won't live past the age of 40.

Relatives also rely on you to help them sort out their problems. Sometimes it's a bit boring listening to grouchy, upset people, but you do your best to be patient. Since formal law courts don't exist yet, you meet with the other village elders to settle serious problems that cannot be cleared up within the family.

A FARMER'S YEAR

In the early 1900s, Irish archeologist R.A.S. Macalister found an ancient stone tablet at Gezer, near present-day Ramla in Israel. The tablet describes, in Hebrew, a farmer's year in the tenth century BCE, beginning in the fall.

Two months
Olive harvesting

Two months
Planting grain

Two months
Late planting

One month
Hoeing flax

One month
Barley harvesting

One month
Harvesting and feasting

Two months
Tending grapevines and picking grapes

One month
Summer fruit harvesting

Senior Homemaker

It's your job to teach your daughters and granddaughters how to cook, bake, tend a vegetable garden, spin yarn, weave cloth, twist plant fibers into rope, and milk goats and sheep. If no midwives live close by, you may help with the delivery of the village babies, too. You also pass down your recipes for root and plant remedies that help sick people feel better. (Even today, grandmothers often treat cold symptoms with a bowl of chicken soup or a cup of herbal tea.) For more serious illnesses, Israelite villagers turned to priests and prophets, in the belief that only Yahweh (God) could cure the sick. Most people didn't begin going to doctors with their health problems until the second century BCE.

OLD-STYLE REAL ESTATE

Each age and continent has its own popular house style. North American pioneers built log cabins, and ancient Mesoamericans put up adobe houses. The Israelites and some of their neighbors built "pillared" houses.

If real-estate agents had existed back then, here's what they might have said about these two-story dwellings:

• Stone pillars divide a large middle room from two smaller side rooms, with a separate room running along the back of the house — ideal for your big family.
• Plastered mud-brick exterior sits on a solid stone foundation.
• Open-plan central room (ideal for preparing food) has well-beaten earthen floor.
• House has lots of storage space — enough to store six months' worth of food! Several circular stone-lined and plastered pits in the back room will keep your family's grain safe from pesky mice and rats.
• Two side rooms have cobbled floors for use as stables. Built-in stone mangers between the pillars will hold feed for your animals. Bonus: Their body heat will keep house warm on cold winter nights.
• Tiny windows keep house cool in summer, let in light, and let out smoke from central room's fire pit.
• Wooden door has the latest Egyptian lock.
• Several niches in the walls will hold oil lamps.
• Interior ladder leads to living and sleeping area on second floor. Exterior ladder provides easy access to roof — a great place for sleeping or entertaining on hot summer nights.
• Outdoor courtyard for cooking with bake oven is included.

Plowman

Even by your time in history, the plow was thousands of years old. Sometime in the distant past, a tired farmer using a wooden hoe to break up the earth before sowing his crop must have thought, "There has to be a better way to do this lousy job." He tried tying a version of the hoe to an animal and — perhaps to his surprise — it worked.

After the first rains in the late fall have softened the stony ground, you hitch up your family's "scratch plow" to a team of oxen. Its iron plow-point scratches narrow furrows up and down the field. Once you have finished sowing, you quickly plow the field again at right angles to the furrows, to cover the seed and protect it from hungry birds and animals. Then, like your neighbor plowing his own family's field nearby in the valley, you pray for more rain.

Animal Trainer

"I'm bored," said the ox to the farmer. "Can I pull your plow?" In your dreams! Everybody knows most steer (neutered male cattle) would much rather chomp their way through a field than drag a plow across one.

Now that you're 10, your father has given you a calf to train. Because the calf is shorter than you are, he will respect you as the dominant animal. By the time he is full-grown and ready to pull a plow, he will follow commands without hesitation, but only if you do your job well. Here are a few tips: Holding your calf's lead rope, say "Giddy-up," lightly tap him on his rump with your stick, and walk ahead. Next, say "Whoa," tap him on his head, and stop. Praise him when he follows your commands, and don't ignore bad behavior. If you are patient and take good care of your future ox, he will respect you and serve your family well.

Terrace Builder

How does building walls make you an early geologist? In the highlands where you live, the limestone and dolomite bedrock forms natural steps in the hills. After you and the other men in your Israelite village have cleared the trees on a slope to make room for vegetable plots, olive groves, orchards, or vineyards, you look for these steps to use as the foundation for your terrace wall. You build the wall across the hillside, using large triangular stones as anchors and smaller stones piled between them. Other men fill the area behind the wall with layers of gravel and soil until they've built up a narrow, level planting area.

In your area's dry, hot climate, terraces help collect rainwater and keep nutrient-rich topsoil from washing off down the hill. Many workers are needed after the harvest to maintain old terraces and build new ones. One historian believes that the number of hours needed to build ancient Israel's highland terraces over many generations would be about the same as the number needed to erect the Egyptian pyramids.

"For, lo, the winter is past, the rain is over and gone;
   The flowers appear on the earth; the time of the singing of birds is come, and the voice of the turtle[dove] is heard in our land;
   The fig tree putteth forth her green figs, and the vines with the tender grape give a good smell."
— Song of Solomon 2:11–13

Sheepshearer

Shepherd

Cheer up! You'll be much cooler after a trim.

Giving sheep a haircut is easier in your day than in previous times, thanks to the invention of iron shears, or scissors. You're proud of your ability to clip about 25 sheep a day — you're faster than the other young men who are shearing their family flocks nearby.

Shearing takes place once a year, in the spring, and is followed by a festival. What better time to throw a wild and woolly party to celebrate your family's good fortune? The rainy winter is over. Wildflowers bloom in the valleys and up the hillsides. And the clan is together. After working hard all day — the men shearing, the women gathering up the wool — everyone is looking forward to an evening of singing, dancing, eating, and drinking.

Your fat-tailed Awassi sheep may look as woolly as the sheep from northern lands, but they are better at keeping their cool. Their dark heads protect them from the summer sun, as does their habit of sticking their noses into the shade under their flockmates' bellies. A thermal barrier between their fleece and their skin, a low pulse rate, and panting also help keep your sheep comfortable. As for those plump tails, when the grazing is poor, your rams and ewes can live on the fat stored in them.

So why do your sheep need you? You and your sheepdog lead the flock to fallow or harvested fields and orchards, where they eat weeds and fertilize the soil with their dung. You also pour fresh water for them into the troughs at the village well and protect them from wild animals. While the sheep are munch, munch, munching, with your dog poised to stop them if they stray, you keep busy spinning yarn from a clump of wool with your spindle.

Hired Hand

After pitching your family's goat-hair tent beside a field, you ask the farmer who has hired you what work he would like you to do. You're a nomad or pastoralist, a landless worker who moves from place to place with his herd. In return for your labor at harvest time, you receive food for your family and grazing rights for your flock of sheep and goats.

During the grain harvest, you're a harvester and sheaf collector. Swinging your curved sickle, you cut the stalks of barley or wheat. Then you scoop the stalks into large sheaves (bundles tied with a few stalks) and load them onto a donkey cart for transport to the village threshing floor. (The "floor" is a large, flat outdoor area.) It's hot, tiring work, made even less pleasant by the cloud of tiny flies that won't leave you alone. At the end of the day, you look forward to returning to the cool interior of your mobile home.

Threshing Sledge Operator

The village fields have produced a good crop of barley this year. Other workers have laid out the stalks on the threshing floor. Once you've hitched up your sledge to a team of oxen or donkeys, you're ready to have a smashing good time. Stone teeth set in the sledge's thick wooden boards do the actual threshing — separating the grain from the stalks. Afterwards, you help your hired hand winnow the grain, tossing it up into the air so that the wind blowing in from the desert can carry away the chaff, leaving the heavier kernels behind.

Everyone in the village helps at harvest time. At the midday meal of bread dipped in wine vinegar, you all talk about the celebration and feast that will follow your hard work.

Slinger

You could give yourself a fancier title than "slinger" if you like. How about "protector of the grape" or "bird avenger"? Your father has sent you out to the vineyards to keep the birds, foxes, and wild boars from feasting on the ripening grapes. He's taught you how to use a slingshot. It doesn't really matter if you hit anything — just launching a stone at a pest drives it off. Practicing with your slingshot is good training for hunting or serving in the militia when you're older, and much more fun than weeding around the vines.

On your way home at sunset, don't forget to pick a bunch of grapes that have ripened early on the south-facing slope. Your mother wants you to bring them home for your family's evening meal of vegetable and lentil stew, yogurt, and bread.

Grape Treader

Clomp, stomp, and mash. Extracting the juice from your family's grape harvest in August and September is the ultimate squishy job. What could be more fun than jumping up and down barefoot on the masses of grapes piled on the *gat*, the stone treading floor of the outdoor wine press?

The more you and the other boys skip and slide, the more juice flows down through a channel into the collecting basin below. The adults pour the juice into jars and store it in a cool place so it can ferment into wine. Later, they pour water over the remains of the grapes to make vinegar or a weak wine for the poor.

Gat it?

Date Picker

Every day toward the end of the summer, you have a date with a bunch of dates. At dawn, you leave your house in the Jordan River Valley and walk to your family's date palm grove. When you first began climbing the scaly trunks of the trees, the bark hurt your hands and feet, but now you're used to it. (To make the climbing easier, your father has scooped out footholds on the oldest fifty-footers.) Once you reach the fruit at the top, you shake each bunch, causing the ripe dates to fall to the ground — pitter-patter. Or you cut off the entire bunch and let it drop — CRASH.

After your younger sisters and brothers have collected the dates on the ground, your mother will dry them or make them into a "honey" (syrup) or wine. No part of the date palm is left unused. The leaves are woven into ropes, baskets, and mats, the wood of old trees that no longer produce fruit becomes lumber, and the seeds are soaked and fed to farm animals when the grazing is poor.

A DATE IGNORES ITS FATE

The towering date palm groves that covered the Jordan River Valley during the Iron Age disappeared over time. Today the valley's date palms are a different species imported from California. In 2005, though, botanist Elaine Solowey planted a seed that came from an extinct palm tree. Archeologists had found it on Mount Masada near the Dead Sea. The 2,000-year-old seed sprouted in a pot! Scientists nicknamed the young tree Methuselah, after the oldest man in the Bible.

BACK FROM THE WILD

In the second century CE (Common Era), many descendants of the dogs used to herd and guard sheep in Old Testament times became "pariah" dogs. They lived in the wild, often in desert areas, because their Israelite masters had died or been forced into exile during a revolt against the Roman Empire.

In the 1930s, the offspring of these smart, sturdy outcasts were redomesticated in Israel. Since then they have worked as guards, herders, trackers, and guides for the blind. The Canaan dog is now Israel's national dog breed. Yip-yip-hurray! Who's a pariah now?

Bread Maker

There's a reason archeologists don't find forks or spoons in Iron Age digs. People living in your time use their fingers to eat, or they scoop up thick vegetable stews from the communal serving bowl with your product — flatbread. Today's pitas and tortillas are examples of this ancient "unleavened" type of bread.

As in many cultures around the world, grinding grain into flour and making bread are jobs for women — two of the many chores that keep you busy for nearly 10 hours each day. Every evening you grind barley kernels between two basalt stones in preparation for the next morning's baking. Bread provides half of your family's daily calories. To feed a family of six, you need to spend about three hours milling. Let's hope you have some help!

Dung Fuel Maker

Unlike people of the future, you don't waste animal waste. To make fuel for your family's bread oven, or *tabun*, you mix farm animal dung with straw, shape the mixture into flat cakes, and dry the cakes in the sun. Don't worry: not even the smoke from the fuel comes into contact with the bread. When the fuel is dry, you pile it against the outside wall of the pottery oven. Once your grandmother lights the dung, the pebble floor inside the oven will grow hot enough to bake the bread dough that's been placed on top of it.

Where do you and your family go to the bathroom? Archeologists have several theories about that. You might head out into a field and do your business there. Inside your home, you might use a large pottery bowl called a krater, which is emptied outside each day. Or you might pay a visit to the stable on the first floor of your house. (What's another dropping in the straw?) Only wealthy city residents have stone toilets built over plaster-lined pits.

Water Hauler

In doing your job, you share a daily task with other girls and women throughout the ancient world. You carry water from the village well to your home. The well is where everyone gathers to hear the latest news. As you wait your turn to lower the wide-mouthed clay jar down into the well by rope, you chat with your friends and neighbors about who is getting married, who is pregnant (having many children was considered a blessing), and who is behind in her weaving.

To carry the water home, you balance the jar on your head. This uses less muscular energy than carrying the same amount of weight on your back. Putting your toes down before your heel as you walk helps you keep your balance and steadies the load. You're lucky that your village well is close by. Some women must walk more than 3 miles (5 km) to the nearest spring, fill goatskin sacks with water, and load them onto their donkey for the trip home. As it is, you have to make several trips to the well to fill the large storage jars set beside the doorway of your house.

"CISTERN, HOW'S IT FLOWING? WELL, THANK YOU."

By the end of the long dry season each year in the Bible Lands, springs and streams had become trickles or dried up completely. Instead of relying on these water sources, ancient people dug wells — deep shafts that tapped into underground springs or aquifers. They also collected rainwater in bottle-shaped reservoirs dug into the rock. The narrow opening of these "cisterns" helped keep the stored water from evaporating.

CHAPTER 2

ROYAL JOBS

Why did the Israelites and their neighbors have kings? Just as the father in each family acted as its leader and protector, the king acted as the father of his kingdom or city-state. The southern Israelite kingdom of Judah, for example, was known as the House of David. Mind you, with flickering oil lamps for light, no flush toilets, and windows without glass panes, an actual royal house of this era would not look anything like today's royal residences. The king's subjects, though, admired the palace's thick stone walls, carved furniture, many rooms, and plant-filled courtyards, all surrounded by a towering wall that set it apart from the city.

Being a member of the royal family and living in a palace had its pluses and minuses. On the positive side: you didn't have to work in the fields, you learned how to read and write, you could play games with your friends on ivory game boards, you slept on a bed rather than a sleeping mat on the floor, and you could stroll in a lovely garden with a servant holding a parasol over your head to protect you from the sun. On the negative side: people depended on the king and other palace folks to do a good job of running the kingdom or city-state and protecting it from danger. It was a big responsibility.

King

No ruler wants to have his good deeds forgotten after he dies, so you are working with a royal scribe to record the history of your kingdom. You're certain that your book will be read and admired by future generations. But what to include?

Here are some questions to get you started. Have you had any beautiful temples built since you became king? As the highest priest in the kingdom, you're expected to do this as a way of honoring the god or gods, depending on your people's beliefs. Have you served your people well? In exchange for the taxes they pay and their labor on your projects and farms, you're expected to help them lead prosperous lives and to protect them from invading armies. Speaking of armies, have you won any wars lately? As the leader of the military, you of course take all the credit for victories on the battlefield.

And a final question: have you proven yourself as a businessman? Everyone barters in the ancient world, even kings. In the ninth and eighth centuries BCE, King Solomon traded Israel's olive oil and grain to King Hiram of Tyre in exchange for Phoenicia's carved ivorywork and cedar. Don't forget to give your fellow king a nice gift to seal the deal. Arranging for the marriage of your daughter to his son wouldn't be a bad idea either.

Court Scribe

Do you like writing and reading out loud? In this important job, you do both. You take down the king's orders, write letters for him, keep financial records, and read his subjects' letters to him. You see these letters first. Sometimes the letter writer will ask you to take the message "with good words" to the king. This is code for "Please read my letter slowly and carefully so that the king will give the matter it discusses serious thought." The king could read the letter himself, of course, but why bother when you're around to do it for him?

...and then I single-handedly captured the enemy fortress...

"You loll on beds inlaid with ivory and lounge on your couches; you feast on lambs from the flock and stall-fed calves;
You improvise on the lute and like David invent musical instruments;
You drink wine by the bowlful and anoint yourselves with the richest oils."
— Amos 6:4–6

Scribe's Apprentice

Very few people of your time learn to read more than a few simple words or measurements. You're one of the lucky ones. Your father is a scribe. He is teaching you himself, but he could also have sent you to a scribal school to learn his trade.

When you're not practicing your writing, you help out in your father's office. You prepare the beeswax that will be spread on the hinged wooden writing boards (they open like modern double photo frames). Then you set out the metal-pointed stylus your father uses for writing on the wax surface. He erases any mistakes with the stylus's flat end. Scribes also use a stylus to write on metal and clay.

No scribe's toolkit is complete without a chisel for stone surfaces, such as monuments, and pens made from reeds. The pens are used for writing with ink on tanned leather or the paper-like papyrus — the most expensive materials. As a scribal student, you often practice with the cheapest materials available: your finger in the dirt.

King's Chief Bodyguard

Chosen personally by the king for your loyalty and bravery, you are a soldier in charge of the palace guard. You and your men must protect your ruler at all costs, particularly on the battlefield, where he is a prime target of the enemy. To do this, you must be a skilled swordsman and train your guards well. Your king's life depends on it.

Here's a test to see if you're the right person for this job. If a lion is about to attack the king, do you: a) run away and hide in your room; b) kill the animal as quickly as possible; or c) call the zoo to tell them their lion is having dinner out? If you answered a) or c), you should look for another line of work.

Hey! This is just practice!

Royal Seal Bearer

Although the monk seal is now one of the world's endangered mammals, in your time it swam along the Mediterranean coastline gobbling up fish and shellfish. You'll be happy to hear that in this job you don't have to lug one around. The king doesn't own a performing pet seal. His is a seal of a different kind: his name or symbol carved into a precious stone and used as a royal stamp of approval.

As a high official, you have earned the trust of the king. Because envelopes don't exist yet, documents written on papyrus or tanned leather are rolled up and the scroll tied with string. You act in the king's name as you stamp royal documents. You place a blob of soft clay on the knot in the string and press the royal seal into the clay. The seal must be broken by the person receiving it before the document can be read.

HOUSE OF THE BULLAE

Did the Israelites have a special house just for bullies? Before you get too excited — who *wouldn't* like to keep bullies in one place? — a *bulla* is the stamped clay disc used to seal scrolls. A government building dating to the seventh or early sixth centuries BCE, uncovered in the City of David excavations in Jerusalem, contained more than 50 *bullae*. The scrolls themselves rotted away long ago, but the Hebrew letters on the *bullae* — many are names found in the Bible — are still readable today.

IRON AGE SCRAP PAPER

In the Iron Age, people cooked, served, and stored their food in pottery bowls and jars. They used pieces of broken pottery as back scratchers and all-purpose scoops in the kitchen. However, the best-known use of pottery shards was as a writing surface for messages, notes, receipts, and students' practice writing. Archeologists call these pottery messages from the past *ostraca*.

Provincial Governor

Inventory Clerk

Today's inventory clerks keep track of the goods delivered by truck to their company's warehouse. They count the supplies, enter the numbers on a computer, and prepare a report at the end of each day. Not much has changed over thousands of years. As each sack-laden donkey or ox-pulled wagon arrives at the royal storehouse, you count the goatskin sacks or jars in the shipment and write down the total and the sender's name on a piece of broken pottery. Later in the day, you collect the pottery fragments in a basket and take them to the accounting office. There you dip your reed pen into a bowl of water, mush it around on a charcoal ink block, and make a permanent record of the day's shipments on a sheet of papyrus.

Having doubts about this job? Count yourself lucky. You could be the sweaty worker hauling the goods into the storehouse.

King Solomon divided his kingdom into provinces to make it easier to collect taxes. The taxes support the royal household, the priesthood, the army, and officials like you.

As provincial governor, you live with your family in a fine house in the center of the regional capital. The officials who work for you visit the villages in your province collecting taxes in the form of grain, cattle, wine, oil, and other goods. As governor, you are responsible for keeping records of what is collected, arranging to have it stored in silos and buildings, and having it delivered by wagon where needed. You are also in charge of the small forts in your region that protect the kingdom's borders and major roads.

Queen

> Tell the scribe I need her at once.

> Yes, Ma'am.

You could just lie around all day in your pretty clothes and jewelry, listening to the court musicians, and stuffing figs in your mouth, but you won't. Your Israelite mother trained you better than that. Raising your children, praying and burning offerings of fragrant oils at a special palace altar, giving orders to palace servants, and writing letters with the help of a scribe keep you very busy.

Another of your duties is acting as a counselor to the king. He depends on you for advice, particularly concerning your children. For example, your husband may ask you which of your sons you think would be best suited to rule after his death. Although the eldest son usually succeeds to the throne, a younger son may sometimes be chosen in his place. If the king dies and the crown prince is too young to rule, you may step in as regent, a very powerful position. With the help of palace officials, you will govern the kingdom until your son is old enough to take on the job.

Yogurt Maker

With no refrigerators, milk spoils quickly in a mild climate. As a servant in the royal household, one of your jobs is to milk the royal nanny goats and make yogurt from the milk.

No smart goat will let you milk her without getting a reward. Before you begin, gently wipe Nanny's udder with a cloth soaked in warm water, and then give her some weeds to munch on while you're milking. When you're finished, take away the clay pot quickly before Nanny kicks it over and you're left crying over spilt milk.

To make yogurt (*lebben*), you fill a goatskin pouch with the fresh milk and some buttermilk and hang it outside overnight. By morning, the milk will have soured and turned into yogurt. You also know how to make butter and *labneh*, a soft cheese that looks like today's cottage or feta cheese.

IF YOU CAN'T BEAT THEM, EAT THEM

Locusts (grasshoppers) could devour cereal crops in great swarms, but they were also a popular crunchy treat. After removing their wings and peeling off their hard shells, people roasted them on sticks over a fire.

Royal Cook

In preparation for celebrating the New Moon, the first day of the lunar month, the palace servants have placed the royal banquet table under the trees in the garden. They have set it with gold bowls for eating and drinking. As the Israelite king's guests arrive, their servants deliver food to you in the kitchen area off the palace's courtyard. Although the guests are honored to be invited to eat with the royal family, they must bring their own food as gifts. You and your helpers are cooking it all up.

You stir a meat stew simmering in a large clay pot over the fire. Unlike ordinary people, the royal family and their friends can afford to eat meat often, not just on feast days. They can also afford exotic spices, the freshest fish, and the finest fruits, nuts, and vegetables. As the servers carry trays of food out to the table, you make sure that they offer the guests spiced wine as well as juice squeezed from the pomegranates grown in the royal orchard. Once the meal is over, you supervise the cleaning up, nibbling on a leftover fig and listening as a group of musicians entertains the guests.

Oh yummy, Esther! Your fig and olive dip is delicious.

Provincial Corvée Official

C'mon, let's get to work over in the King's field.

You're not a popular guy: *corvée* means "work gang." Beginning under King Solomon's reign, you order villagers in your province to work for the government. Today governments use our taxes to hire people to build roads and public buildings. In the Iron Age, men were expected to toil for a few months a year on royal construction projects or plowing or harvesting the royal fields. No one wants to be taken from their own jobs to slave away on government jobs, so don't expect any thanks for the work you do as the king's official.

Head Gardener

When you were younger, you might have agreed with the Egyptian writer who wrote in 1800 BCE, "The gardener works himself to death, more than all other professions." Not anymore. You leave the dirty work to your team of assistant gardeners and laborers.

The palace grounds are called a "pleasure garden" because they overflow with colorful flowers, tasty herbs, shade trees, vines, and different varieties of fruit and nut trees. On hot, dusty days, you enjoy the rare privilege in an arid land of strolling along cool, shady walkways.

The garden serves a useful purpose, too. You and your staff pick herbs for the royal family's meals and harvest fruit, nuts, and grapes as they ripen. You also make sure that workers clean out the irrigation channels regularly and keep the garden's pools stocked with fish. As well as being fun to watch and good to eat, the fish gobble up mosquito larvae. A pleasure garden isn't a pleasure if buzzing swarms attack its visitors.

CHAPTER 3

CITY JOBS

A smelly place packed with people scurrying about, delivery vehicles blocking the road, and workers fixing the water-supply system — an Iron Age city sounds strangely familiar. But that's where the similarities to a modern city end. In size, an ancient city had the same number of residents as today's town. It looked different, too. A high wall with gatehouses and towers surrounded its two-story buildings, which were clustered together on narrow streets. When an enemy army surrounded and attacked a city, the wall protected the people inside — at least for a while. If the siege lasted for a long time and their king refused to surrender, those trapped inside could slowly starve. In an Israelite city the main gatehouse, with one to three rooms on either side of the gate, stood on the road leading to a public square. In peacetime, the city's elders held meetings in these rooms and merchants traded goods in a bazaar nearby.

Over the course of the Iron Age, numerous cities in the Bible Lands were founded and destroyed. Some were rebuilt and others abandoned. Cities of the time included the bustling ports and colonies of the Phoenicians, the manufacturing hubs of the Philistines, and the royal cities and administrative and military centers of the Israelites.

City Governor

Today you would be called the mayor. As a high government official in a royal city, you are in charge of the city's finances — the collection of taxes — as well as the building projects and repairs that taxes make possible. A king wouldn't appear very kinglike to his people if he lived in a shabby city or couldn't protect his subjects from danger, so it's your job to keep up appearances.

You and your fellow citizens are used to being walled in. Because the royal city must be particularly well guarded, you've ordered your staff to install the latest security system — a casemate wall. Unlike the Bronze Age solid wall, this is a double wall with enough space between the two to create rooms for storage or living quarters. (At Be'er Sheva, an ancient city in southern Israel, these casemate rooms served as the back rooms of row houses on a ring road.) You might also think about adding a dry moat, a deep ditch around the city, to make your casemate wall harder for enemy soldiers to scale.

PIECES OF SILVER

Although silversmiths turned silver into jewelry, statuettes, and bowls, people also used this precious metal as a form of money. The silver *shekel* wasn't a coin, though. It was a measurement of weight.

The Philistines, Phoenicians, and Israelites weighed small pieces of silver on a scale, two metal pans hung from a bar. They put the silver in one pan and enough small stone or metal weights in the other to balance the two. Weights ranged from the *talent* (equal to 3,000 shekels) to the *gerah* (20 gerahs equaled one shekel). Later, the shekel did become a coin, and today it is the monetary unit of Israel.

Chief Gatekeeper

You supervise the numerous gatekeepers needed in a royal city, which has several entrances. Like border guards today, gatekeepers control who enters the city. As the boss, you make sure that the thick wooden double doors are always manned, that your gatekeepers are well trained and armed, and that the doors are closed at night and bolted from the inside with a heavy beam. The gates are the weakest part of a city's defense system. It's your job to keep them well protected.

Innkeeper

Pilgrims visiting the temple, foreign traders, merchants, and travelers who don't have family living in the city stay at your small inn. Making people feel welcome was important in ancient Israel. When your guests first walk through your door, you invite them to remove their sandals and wash their feet in the pottery basin in the corner. This doesn't make you one of those people who nag others about washing behind their ears. Inviting your guests to wash their feet is both good manners and good sense. Here's why.

Your neighbors sweep the dirt from their floors into the street, and they toss their garbage there, too. Since several thousand people live in the city, the dirt piles up. Donkeys and stray dogs leave their stinky deposits in the streets as well. Rain in the wet season eventually washes the mess away, but not before your guests have walked through what's left of it.

Fowler

Ordinary people in your era didn't eat meat every day. Any they did eat, on feast days or at weddings or other special occasions, came mainly from the sheep and goats they raised. However, hunters also killed deer and other wild animals for food. They were familiar with the migration routes of birds, too. The hunters set out nets in the marshes to catch ducks and geese, captured partridges in traps, and shot other birds with bows and arrows.

In your shop in the bazaar, you are a middle-man between the villagers who bring you domestic chickens, eggs, and the wild birds they have killed and the city dwellers who can afford to buy them. The only "foul" part of your job is handling the dead "fowl," or birds, that you sell. A butcher down the street sells cuts of meat.

"Deliver thyself as a roe from the hand of the hunter, and as a bird from the hand of the fowler."
— Proverbs 6:5

Wine Shop Owner

People who were hot and thirsty in biblical times couldn't just get a drink from a public water fountain. Even if drinking fountains had existed, it wouldn't have been smart to use one. Water was often polluted, which is one reason wine was the most popular drink in ancient Israel.

You buy the wine for your shop from the winery at Gibeon (el-Jib), northwest of Jerusalem. The town was a major center for making and exporting wine in the ninth and eighth centuries BCE. It was famous for its dozens of wine cellars cut into the solid rock. These kept the wine, stored in jars, at a constant cool temperature. Wineries sometimes shipped the wine overland by cart in a human-sized ceramic vessel called a pithos.

At your store, you have a "bring your own bowl" policy. You dip a small pottery container, a "juglet," into one of your wine storage jars and pour the wine into your customers' drinking bowls.

Baker

You and your family bake wheat bread and honey cakes for wealthy customers. (The poor eat barley bread.) Early each morning, you add water to flour, along with a bit of salt and a little "starter," a piece of fermented, or sour, dough from the previous day's bread batch. The yeast in the starter leavens (puffs up) the dough. While you shape the dough into balls and let them rise, your eldest daughter lights the stick-and-straw fire in the bottom of the *tannûr*, a beehive-shaped clay oven.

Then comes the "do-this-fast-or-burn-your-fingers" part. You flatten the dough balls into discs, reach through a hole in the oven's top, and slap each disc onto the hot inner walls of the *tannûr*. The discs will bake in less than a minute. To store your fresh bread, you string it on a stick hung from the ceiling, out of the reach of mice and rats. Some scholars think the Hebrew word *matteh-lehem* ("staff of life") may refer to this bread pole rather than to the bread itself.

Olive Oil Maker

Olive grove owners harvest their crop in September and October. They beat the branches of their trees with long sticks, collect the fallen olives in baskets and bring them to you for processing. You own one of the new beam-presses invented during the second half of the Iron Age. Your workers produce the best oil, or virgin oil, by rolling a large stone over the olives in a crushing basin, adding hot water, and then skimming off the oil that floats to the surface. (Even today, people are willing to pay more for the better-tasting first-pressed oil.) After draining the basin, the workers scoop the pulp that is left behind into baskets and squeeze the baskets in the beam-press to extract the second-grade oil.

You and your fellow oil men sell your liquid gold to Egypt; olive trees don't grow there. Between 1981 and 1996, archeologists found more than 100 presses at Tel Miqne, the remains of the Philistine city of Ekron. They estimate 500 tons of oil may have flowed each year out of Ekron into the eager markets of the Near East. Why so much? Ancient people didn't just cook with olive oil. They used it to fuel lamps, to treat cuts, as an ingredient in cosmetics and perfumes, and as an offering in their temples.

Colonial Governor

Elissa, the sister of a Phoenician king, is said to have founded the city of Carthage in North Africa in 814 BCE. When she arrived in the region with a group of people from Tyre, the local inhabitants agreed to sell the colonists a piece of land only as large as an ox-hide would cover. The sneaky Elissa sliced the hide into very skinny strips and encircled an entire hill.

The ox-hide trick is probably a local legend by the time you govern Carthage. Carthage, which means New City (from the Phoenician *qart*, "city," and *hadasht*, "new"), is no longer new. It's the leading Phoenician colony. As its governor, you control trade in the western Mediterranean. You and your clerks and scribes keep track of the metals and other raw materials and goods flowing through your port and on to Phoenicia. Unfortunately for future archeologists, no sign of your hard work survives. The Romans burned all the city's records when they destroyed Carthage in 146 BCE.

CHAPTER 4

BUILDING AND DIGGING JOBS

I sraelites and their neighbors may not have built the towering cathedrals or impressive palaces of later ages, but they made good use of local materials — clay, straw, wood, and particularly stone. They erected elegant temples and government buildings using the region's limestone, and they dug down into the bedrock to carve out underground tombs, mine shafts, wine cellars, and tunnels.

Visitors wading through Hezekiah's Tunnel in Jerusalem can still see the marks of the workers' pickaxes on the walls of the eighth-century BCE water tunnel. The tunnel isn't impressive to look at — it's only 2 feet (0.6 m) wide — but at 583 yards (533 m) long, it's a remarkable engineering feat for its time. More than a century after the tunnel's discovery in 1880, archeologists still don't know exactly how the workers made their way through the rock from opposite ends to meet in the middle.

Brick Maker

Everything has its season — even mud. For brick making, you collect clay in May or June, after the spring rains. It's easier to dig then. Straw, your second raw ingredient, is also plentiful in the late spring. After mixing the clay and cut-up straw, you pack the mixture into rectangular wooden forms and place the molds in the sun to dry.

Since one scholar has guessed that you need 132 pounds (60 kg) of straw to manufacture 100 mud bricks, you might be tempted to skip the straw. Don't. Dried mud has good compressive strength (it presses together well) while straw has good tensile strength (it stretches well). Combined, the two make an excellent material for constructing houses and other buildings — in fact, bricks are the most popular building material in the Bible Lands.

Planning Engineer

What's 300 cubits long, 50 cubits wide, and 30 cubits high? Noah's ark. But just how big *is* that? As an engineer in the city planning office, you would know. The royal cubit, an Egyptian measure used throughout the ancient Mediterranean, is the distance from a man's elbow to the tip of his middle finger, about 21 inches (53 cm). Using parts of the body as units of measure was common in early civilizations. Today a horse's height is still measured in "hands," the width of a man's palm.

City engineers draw up street plans, measure building sites with wooden measuring rods and ropes, and supervise the construction of gates, storehouses, stables, forts, and other public buildings. How does your work measure up? Even with the primitive tools and building methods of your time, the remains of some of your buildings are still around thousands of years later.

Logger

As a logger, you don't cut down just any old tree. The trees you fell are the towering cedars that grow in the mountains of Phoenicia (today's Lebanon). They are famous throughout the eastern Mediterranean region for their long-lasting wood.

You work with another axman as a team. While you take turns swinging your axes, two other loggers hold ropes they've tied high up on the trunk and looped around a nearby tree.

When the cedar is about to fall, they will guide its path so that its branches don't get caught in another tree.

You use oxen to drag the logs out of the forest. In the spring, the timber will be floated down a river to the Mediterranean Sea. From there, it will be loaded onto ships or towed behind them on rafts to Israel or Egypt. King David's and King Solomon's temples and palaces were all said to be built with the cedar of Lebanon.

"And the ruler ... supplied **300 men and 300 oxen, and he appointed supervisors in charge of them, to have them fell the lumber. And they felled it. And they spent the winter at it.**"
— Wenamun, an Egyptian official who traveled by sea to the Phoenician town of Byblos around 1075 BCE to buy wood for the Pharaoh

Carpenter

Most villagers are handy with an ax. They shape tree trunks into rough roof beams for new houses. They make window and door frames as well as ladders, looms, and simple tools. In the city, though, you must be a skilled carpenter if you want to make your living putting up temples or public buildings.

First, you must be familiar with the different types of wood —juniper, pine, oak, cedar, and acacia — and know where you can buy them for the best price. Second, you must know how to measure with a wooden ruler and how to use a saw, an awl (a pointy tool for making small round holes), a bow drill (a tool that twists into wood to make large round holes), and a chisel. Finally, both you and the stone mason you work with must know how to prevent the temple or house you're building from falling down in an earthquake.

Yes, thousands of years ago builders practiced earthquake-proofing. (Quakes occur along the region's Dead Sea fault zone.) They placed wooden beams horizontally between rows of stone blocks in a wall. The wood made the wall less rigid and better able to absorb shock waves.

Stone Mason

You are very good at dressing. No, that doesn't mean you can put on your loincloth in 10 seconds flat, although maybe you can. "Dressing" a piece of limestone means to shape it with a chisel (a narrow piece of iron with a sharp edge) into a large block with six smooth sides. After you dress the blocks at the construction site, you and your crew build a house with them for your client, a powerful official.

You are so good at chiseling off the bumps from your ashlar blocks that they fit together almost as tightly as today's interlocking toy bricks. You don't even use mortar to stick them together. Simply alternating blocks with their short sides facing out and blocks with their long sides facing out is enough to keep your walls from tumbling down.

Plaster Maker

Your job is truly ancient. People first made plaster in the Near East around 7000 BCE, before they made iron or even pottery. In the Iron Age, your customers depend on your product to keep water in *and* to keep water out. A coating of plaster on underground cisterns and reservoirs prevents stored rainwater from seeping away through tiny holes in the rock. Applied to the walls of homes, plaster stops the underlying mud bricks from crumbling in the heavy rains of winter and early spring.

Making plaster takes days of hard labor. To make 1 ton of plaster, you need to collect nearly 2 tons of limestone. Better collect some firewood on your search, too. You'll need 2 tons of it as well. To make the main ingredient of plaster, you heat chunks of limestone in your kiln, a pit lined with stones and topped with a stone dome. Three days of intense heat turn the rock into a powder. Mixing the burned lime with water and sand forms a paste that can be spread on a wall, where it hardens into a waterproof surface.

Dinner, Dad!

ODD JOBS AROUND THE HOUSE

When today's homeowners notice that their roofs need repair, most of them hire a roofer. In the Iron Age, people with the same problem got rolling. After a rainstorm, they would pull a 3-foot-long (1m) stone roller across their flat roofs to reseal the thick layer of plastered clay laid over a layer of branches or reeds.

Grave Robber

Slave Miner

Aren't you just the lowest of the low? No wonder the family of an Israelite royal official had a warning carved over his tomb in the eighth century BCE: "No silver or gold is here. ... Cursed be the man who opens this." But curses don't scare you. Jerusalem is ringed with cemeteries containing tombs — natural caves or underground rooms cut into the rock. Family members place lamps, pottery jars, seals, jewelry, tools, and other items in the tomb for their dead relatives to use in the afterworld. It's easy loot for a creep like you. But if you are caught, you will have to return what you stole to the family and pay a large fine. Robbers who can't do this are sold into slavery.

Are you afraid of the dark, or nervous about climbing up and down ladders, or don't like getting dirty and sweaty? Too bad. As a prisoner of war or a thief sold into slavery, you have no say in what job you do.

Early each morning you wait your turn to climb down a ladder fixed to the wall of the main shaft of the copper mine. Take a big breath of fresh air — the shaft may be very deep. At the bottom, you walk through a tunnel to reach your work area in one of the galleries, or underground rooms. By the dim light of an oil lamp, you use a chisel, hammer, and pickax to remove chunks from the vein of ore. Then you pile the pieces into a large basket. Another slave hauls the basket to the mine shaft, where it is pulled up by rope to the surface.

Stale, dust-choked air, falling rock, and the lack of protective gear make mining dangerous work. No wonder an ancient Greek writer said that the strongest slave miners were the most unfortunate, because they were the slowest to die.

A PET DOG DIGS HIS WAY INTO THE PAST

By 1854, American missionary and scholar Dr. James Turner Barclay had already made several important archeological finds in Jerusalem. But although he had heard rumors of a mysterious cave near the Damascus Gate in the Old City wall, he and his two sons couldn't find an entrance. Their pet dog did. One day it dug its way into a hole that heavy rains had opened at the foot of the wall. When the Barclays followed their dog, they found the entrance to a huge underground quarry and the skeleton of a former visitor! The ancient limestone quarry, which was later called Zedekiah's Cave, had supplied building blocks for the city.

Water Tunnel Miner

In 701 BCE, Hezekiah, king of Judah, ordered his engineers to find a way to protect Jerusalem's water supply during an expected Assyrian attack. The solution they came up with was to build a tunnel that would carry water from the Gihon Spring over 500 yards (450 m) south to the Pool of Siloam, a reservoir inside the city walls. Two crews would dig toward each other from opposite ends and meet in the middle.

You work as a miner with the north crew. For months, the two teams have been digging through the limestone rock underlying the city at a rate of about 6 feet (1.8 m) a day. It's hard to know exactly where you're going, and both teams have dug in the wrong direction several times. That meant backing up and starting again. But today you hear the sound of the other crew's pickaxes, and through a natural crack in the rock, you soon hear their voices, too.

The joining of the two ends of Hezekiah's Tunnel is so exciting that someone records the event on the tunnel wall. The Hebrew inscription reads: "So on the day the breakthrough was made, the pickmen struck, one gang toward the other, pickax against pickax; and the water flowed."

CHAPTER 5

FIERY JOBS

The Iron Age could be called the Age of Fire. As the population of the Bible Lands grew, metalsmiths and glassmakers worked hard to keep up with the demand for new tools, ornaments, and weapons. The objects made in their furnaces changed the way people lived, worked, and fought.

To supply the fuel for furnaces, more trees had to be felled. As the forests shrank, wood became more difficult to find. Smiths and glassmakers competed for fuel with potters, plaster makers, jewelers, bakers, and cooks. Some scholars believe that one reason smiths switched to iron from copper or bronze was that they could produce more metal for the same amount of fuel. Even thousands of years ago, saving fuel was a hot topic.

Charcoal Maker

In your era, people think metalsmiths are magicians. Without charcoal makers like you, the magic wouldn't happen. In his charcoal-fueled furnace, the smith separates metal from ore. The carbon in your charcoal is needed for this chemical change to take place. Charcoal also provides the intense, steady heat necessary for the smelting process.

You learned the secrets of making charcoal from your father. Charcoal is simply chunks of wood set on fire and charred in a closed space. But if you don't stack your fuelwood correctly in the pit where you char it, or cover the pit with enough leaves and earth, or the air flow isn't just right, you'll end up with ashes rather than charcoal. In many developing countries today, charcoal is still used as a household fuel.

ELEPHANTS AND CHARCOAL

The wild elephant herd of Syria is last mentioned in ancient documents from the ninth century BCE. One scholar thinks that the demand for charcoal for iron smelting and tool making may have caused the herd's extinction. Tree branches are the best wood for producing charcoal, but they are also the number one food for elephants. Charcoal workers may have stripped the trees of their branches, leaving the trees to die and the elephants with nothing to eat.

Bronze Arrowhead Maker

Ironmaker

Although you live in the Iron Age, you make arrowheads from the metal that gave its name to the Bronze Age (3000–1200 BCE). Adding tin to copper makes this alloy, which is a harder metal than copper alone.

To start, you place layers of charcoal and copper ore mixed with hematite, an iron ore, in your smelting furnace. You increase the heat of the fire by using bellows to force air through clay pipes in the top, sides, or bottom of the furnace. Unfortunately, you can't raise or lower the furnace's temperature during the smelting process. It's all trial and error. If no puddle of copper appears, you're out of luck and will have to try again.

To make bronze, you remelt the copper with tin in another furnace, and then pour the mixture into molds made in the shape of arrowheads. Someone else probably assembles the arrows, attaching your heads to reed or wood shafts and fixing on feathers to make the arrows fly straight without wobbling. Once you've finished your order of arrows, why not make one of your "hairy" products — razors, tweezers, or hair curlers?

You are a master of fire. However, if you take on this smelting job, you may have to say goodbye to your eyebrows and eyelashes. To make wrought iron, you must heat pieces of iron ore in your charcoal-fueled furnace to 2012°F (1100°C). (That's hot. Water boils at 212°F/ 100°C! However, it's still not hot enough to turn this particular ore into a liquid, allowing you to pour it into a mold and make cast iron. Ironmakers won't be able to do that for another 2,000 years.)

After several hours at 2012°F, the ore separates into a usable spongy mass of metal called the bloom and unusable stuff called slag. You pull the bloom out of the furnace with tongs and reheat it in your forge, an open charcoal fire. Once it is hot enough, you remove the bloom from the flames and hammer it to drive out any bits of slag. More reheating, hammering, and shaping turn the bloom into an ax blade, sword, chisel, points for a plow, or even bracelets.

"The smith with the tongs both worketh in the coals, and fashioneth it with hammers, and worketh it with the strength of his arms."
— Isaiah 44:12

Steelmaker

You make the second-hardest substance on earth, next to a diamond: martensite. How cool is that? In fact, cooling has a lot to do with it.

By the tenth century BCE, you and other smiths know that wrought iron can be hardened into steel by heating it in white-hot charcoal, then dunking it in cold water. After this "quenching," a layer of martensite forms on the iron. This makes your object very hard, but also very brittle. To make it less likely to shatter, you temper it by heating it at a low temperature to reduce some of the martensite in the metal, then quench it again. Since you have no way of measuring the temperature of your fire, your steel weapons and tools are sometimes winners and sometimes duds.

Glassmaker

Glassblowing hasn't been invented yet, so you don't spend your time making clear window-panes or eyeglasses or wineglasses. Instead, you create colorfully decorated vases and vessels using the core-forming method invented by the Egyptians.

You start by packing clay in the shape of the final object around a metal rod. This forms the core. Then you heat wood ashes, limestone, and finely ground sand together in a charcoal-fired furnace until they begin to fuse. (Fortunately for you, sand beaches line the coastline of your homeland, Phoenicia.) You dip the core into the molten glass and swirl it around. After decorating your new container while it is still semi-molten, you roll it on a stone slab to smooth out the surface. Finally, very carefully — very, very carefully — you take out the rod and scrape out the clay core.

CHAPTER 6

CRATS JOBS

Although Iron Age people needed everyday tools and utensils, they liked beautiful objects, just as we do. With simple tools and materials, craftspeople produced exceptional work. The Phoenicians, in particular, stand out. Hemmed in by the Mediterranean and a mountain range, with little usable land to farm, they turned to exporting wood, salting fish, building ships, and making finely crafted items to trade with other peoples. How's that for coming up with solutions to your problems when the times get tough?

Gold Jewelry Maker

In your workshop, twisting gold wires into wrist or ankle bracelets is easy compared to a decorating technique called granulation. For that, you need steady hands and good eyesight; you decorate earrings with patterns of tiny gold balls held in place with glue or resin. To make the granules, you heat small pieces of gold on a charcoal block in your furnace, directing the heat with a blowpipe. As the bits melt, they roll into balls.

Both men and women of the upper class wear your small masterpieces. Like today's owners of fine jewelry, people living during the Iron Age hid their expensive ornaments when they weren't wearing them. Archeologists have found jewelry collections under the floors of ancient homes.

Gold Beater

THUD. THUD. THUD. It's enough to give you a pounding headache. People in the Iron Age thumped or smashed all sorts of things — grain, grapes, iron. As a goldsmith's son, you beat the most valuable metal known: gold imported from Arabia or Egypt. You place a chunk of gold on a flat stone and pound it into a very thin sheet using a round-bottomed hammer stone. Gold is a soft metal. To prevent leaving hammer marks as the gold thins out, you place it between two pieces of leather.

Your father has recently taught you how to make a good impression. You press a sheet of gold over a mold carved with raised shapes, such as flowers, and hammer the gold until the shapes appear on the sheet. As well as pounding out plaques and decorations, you cut fine strips, or wires, from the sheets. Cloth makers weave your glittering wires into the fancy cloth they make for royalty and the priesthood.

"They did beat the gold into thin plates, and cut it into wires, to work it in the blue, and in the purple, and in the scarlet, and in the fine linen, with cunning work."
— Exodus 39:3

Locksmith

Once you've made a lock, you might find it difficult to put its wooden key in your pocket. The key measures 10 to 20 inches (25 to 50 cm) long and looks like today's toothbrush. The "Egyptian" lock it opens is named after the people who first designed it. Just as carpenters use wooden pegs hammered into holes to join two pieces of wood, you use small movable pegs in your tumbler lock. The lock is attached to the inside of a door. When the pegs tumble down into position, they keep a long piece of wood called a bolt in its slot in your customer's door frame.

To unlock the door from the outside, your customer reaches through a hole in the door. He slides the key's "teeth" into position under the matching teeth of the lock, pushes them up into the lock box, and slides the bolt across, opening the door.

A perfect fit is key for a strong lock.

Ivory Carver

You're a copycat, and proud of it. You turn elephant tusks bought from traders into carved decorative panels for wooden footstools, chairs, and beds. Some art critics in the future will call your works of art knockoffs, because although you're Phoenician, you copy Egyptian, Assyrian, and Greek designs. Don't let it bother you. In the ninth century BCE, people throughout the Mediterranean world are proud to own one of your beautiful ivories.

To prepare a tusk for carving, you must first grind away its bony "rind." Then you cut the underlying "dentin" with a saw into strips or cross-sections. After choosing a design from your pattern collection — maybe a warrior fighting a winged creature — you roughly gouge it out on the panel. Only experienced craftsmen like you can chisel the details like the feathers on the beast's wings and the plates on the soldier's armor.

Shell Engraver

Beetle Carver

During the sixth century BCE, you engrave giant clamshells imported from the Red Sea. (The elephants whose tusks craftsmen used to carve have been extinct for generations.) The shape of these shells reminds you of a bird spreading its wings. Before you begin carving, you knock off the bumps on the shell's exterior with a hammer and polish the surface into smooth folds. Then you carve the knob near the hinge of the shell into a falcon's head and decorate the folds with feathers and lotus flowers.

Archeologists today think your half-shells may have been used as pretty containers for cosmetics or jewelry. What girl wouldn't have wanted one in her bedroom?

Why have archeologists found hundreds of *scarabs* — small beetles carved of stone — in ancient Israel? Did people of that time think beetles were cute? Probably not. In Egypt, real scarab-beetles were connected with Re, the sun god. Egyptians made the stone amulets, or good luck charms, for use in their own land and for export, particularly to Canaan, during the Bronze Age. Although the scarab had no place in their world view, Canaanites may have simply liked the exotic jewelry and its reputation for protection against evil.

Beetle mania caught on and lasted for centuries. At some point it attracted the attention of you and your fellow Phoenician stone engravers. You keep the basic Egyptian beetle shape but engrave your own decorations onto your scarabs for export. Thanks to you, scarabs have become popular in ancient Greece, Crete, and Cyprus.

Potter's Apprentice

You're an Iron Age caveman. Your Israelite father set up his pottery workshop in a cave because it's roomy, cool in the summer, and a good place to dry newly made jars before they are fired. (Direct sunlight and wind can crack the clay.) The people of the city nearby keep your father and his assistants busy making offerings for graves (jugs, bowls, and lamps), storage jars, cooking pots, footbaths, and toys in the shape of animals.

You help by grinding red ochre with a mortar, carrying water from the cistern outside, and kneading the clay with your feet. You also help find fuel for the kiln. You're glad your father uses a double potter's wheel in his work; he rotates the top wheel by kicking the lower wheel with his foot. If he used a single potter's wheel, you would be kneeling on the ground spinning it round and round and round all day. Boring!

BABY JARS

Babies and young children were sometimes buried in storage jars during the Iron Age. Sadly, many children died due to polluted water and rotten food.

Archeologists have found "jar burials" in Canaan and Philistia dating from the thirteenth to eleventh centuries BCE. The small, enclosed space of a jar may have reminded the ancients of a mother's womb, just as tombs were built to look like houses. Some researchers also think that children buried this way may have been sacrificed in religious rituals.

Clay Coffin Maker

Bowyer

Why waste your talent making puny jars when you can create containers large enough for a body? Although you are a Philistine, you make pottery coffins in the Egyptian style. You build the mummy-shaped containers using coils of clay, and on the lid of the coffin you sculpt the dead person's face, arms, and hands. Before the coffin is hardened in a large outdoor fire (it's too big for a kiln), you cut out the lid and fire it separately.

In your workshop, you are training your son to be a bowyer, or bow maker. It takes great patience and lots of time to craft a composite bow. First you show him how to select and prepare the weapon's raw materials — wood, horn, strands of sinew pulled from a deer's leg tendon, and glue. You make the bow's wooden "limbs," then glue horn on the side that will be closest to the archer and thin layers of sinew on the other side. Each layer must be set aside to cure, or set, before you can apply the next layer. The entire process can take up to a year.

The combination of the springy horn and elastic sinew makes one very tense bow — and sometimes one very tense bowyer. After all that work, you don't want a clumsy archer stringing your new bow. One false step in stretching its limbs and the bow can twist and break. SPROING! Better string it yourself and hope the archer keeps the bow "braced" — ready to use in its leather bow case.

CHAPTER 7

WHAT-TO-WEAR JOBS

To look your very best in the Bible Lands, you probably can't go wrong with a loose-fitting ankle-length tunic worn with a belt or sash, a cloak that doubles as a blanket at night, a cap or a turban if you're a man, and a shawl or headscarf if you're a woman. Only wealthy people could afford to wear richly embroidered and dyed linen; everyone else made do with wool.

Who did the laundry? Ordinary men and women probably had only one set of woolen clothing, so they didn't clean it often. People in the upper classes, however, would have had more than one outfit, along with the servants and the extra water to wash them.

Weaver
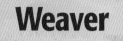

Fuller

Why do you spend a lot of time staring at a wall? Because to weave cloth for clothing, storage bags, and blankets, you must lean your warp-weighted loom up against one. The warp (or vertical) threads are tied onto the loom's top beam and held straight by clay weights attached to their ends. To weave, you use a shuttle to pass the woof (or horizontal) thread over and under the warp threads.

After thousands of years, nothing will remain of your wooden loom or the cloth you made from the spun yarn of sheep's wool or goat's hair. But archeologists have found many clay loom-weights in the remains of ancient houses, so they know you once were there.

If you like splashing around in puddles, you might like this job. Fullers clean wool and woven cloth before it is dyed. To do this, you put the cloth in a large tub of water and march up and down on it, working out natural oils and dirt with your toes. You may also clean the cloth by rubbing it with your version of detergent — natron (natural soda, a salt-like substance found in deposits near lakes) mixed with oil.

Dye Factory Owner

Your purple dye is the only one in the ancient world that won't fade in the wash. It takes great skill to make and is so expensive that only rich people can afford to wear purple clothes.

To make the dye, your workers must first trap many thousands of marine snails every year in straw baskets baited with pieces of fish. At the dyeworks, they break open the large shells and crush the smaller ones to remove a tiny gland containing the precious liquid that will be used to make purple dye. They salt the glands and then cook them in a large pot of water, skimming off the fleshy bits that rise to the surface. That's the easy part. As a master dyer, you must now add special ingredients to the liquid to make it into a dye.

Today you would have a chemistry degree, but in your day you were probably trained by your father. Your hometown, the Phoenician city of Tyre, reeks, thanks to your dye factory. No one turns up their noses, though, at the wealth your business brings to Tyre.

Fibula Maker

No, you don't make fake leg bones, although the fibula leg bone may be named after your product. Here's a clue. Without you, people's clothes might fall off. Still don't know? You are the proud maker of the new metal fibula, or brooch, which looks like today's safety pin.

The fibula fastens cloaks and other pieces of clothing, as well as closing cloth sacks. It's a big improvement over the toggle pin. To do up a cloak with a toggle, you wound a string sewn on one side around a pin sewn on the other. Your fibula is much faster to do up and less likely to break.

Tanner

Most men living in the Iron Age pee against an outside wall or in the fields, but not you. Since you use urine in your work, you probably pee into a clay jar. You soak goat, sheep, or calf hides in the urine to help loosen the hair or wool on one side of the skin and the remaining tissue on the other side. Then you scrape the hide. Animal dung or special plant solutions (tannins) help remove blood, dirt, and any remaining fat and flesh. These smelly mixtures also soften the leather over the months the skins sit in various pits.

Craftspeople use the leather you produce to make sandals, belts, loincloths, helmets, quivers for arrows, and containers for liquids. Hooves, bones, and leftover bits and pieces are boiled down to make glue. Although people want the products your work makes possible, they don't want to be your neighbor. They think your stinky job is unclean, so you're forced to live on the outskirts of town.

EARLY POOL NOODLE

Tanners turned a goatskin into a water bottle by removing the skin whole from the beheaded carcass, being careful not to poke holes in the skin with their knives. They then cleaned it thoroughly and sewed up the neck and leg holes. Ordinary people carried water in these "waterskins." When soldiers or travelers needed to ford a river that was too high to wade across, they sometimes inflated their skins and paddled to the other side on their homemade "noodles."

Sandal Maker

Comb Maker

An old saying, "If it ain't broke, don't fix it," could apply to one of your tools. Many centuries ago Egyptian sandal makers used a knife that was the same shape as yours. Nineteenth-century shoemakers will use it, too. The knife's half-moon blade is just right for slicing the leather in the shape of your customers' feet. After you cut out the soles, or bottoms, of the sandals, you hammer them to make the leather stiff and hard-wearing. Finally you use an awl to poke holes in the sole and attach leather strips for straps.

Ordinary people feel very lucky if they are able to afford a pair of your sandals. Most walk barefoot.

Since both men and women wear their hair long in the Iron Age, everyone needs your product. Not everyone can afford one of your combs, though. You carve each one from a piece of ivory. It's tough work making each little fine tooth, and you're happy when you've completed that part of the comb and can move on to the widely spaced teeth at the other end. You might be surprised to learn that your combo comb design is still being used in the twenty-first century.

Eye Makeup Mixer

Mixing eye makeup for your mistress is just one of your jobs as a maid. First, you collect your tools — a pestle and a round limestone palette with a round depression in the center. Like Egyptian women, your mistress wears something called kohl as an eyeliner to make her eyes look bigger. In the days before sunglasses, kohl also helped protect eyes from the bright sun. To make it, you grind a dark grey ore called galena into a blackish powder.

To apply the kohl, you moisten the end of a small stick, dip it into the powder, then draw a line of kohl along your mistress's eyelids. After your work is done, you hand your mistress a mirror made of polished metal (glass mirrors don't exist yet). If you're lucky, your work will be a real eye opener.

NOT NICE FOR LICE

Parents have been combing nits, or lice eggs, out of their children's hair for thousands of years. The people of the Bible Lands poured olive oil over their children's and their own itchy heads to suffocate the lice and make it easier to comb out the nits.

CHAPTER 8

SPICY, SCENTED JOBS

Today people slap on deodorant, dab on perfume, burn scented candles, and toss spices into their food without thinking about it. No big deal. In the Iron Age, spices and fragrant oils were a very big deal. They were that era's "gotta have" items. To keep up with the demand, South Arabian merchants shipped these exotic goods across the Arabian desert by camel caravan.

Caravaneer

"And [the queen of Sheba] came to Jerusalem with a very great train, with camels that bore spices, and very much gold, and precious stones."
— 1 Kings 10:2

In your era, people travel together in donkey or camel "caravans" as protection against lions, leopards, and other wild animals, as well as bandits and warlords. You're in charge of a camel caravan crossing the Arabian desert. The camels are loaded with frankincense and myrrh, precious resins used to make incense and perfumes.

Camels are called "ships of the desert." Like a modern freighter, a one-humped camel takes advantage of pit stops to gulp down all the fuel (water and desert plants) it needs for the next leg of the long voyage. If you travel in the cool of the desert night, a dromedary can carry about 220 pounds (100 kg) for 37 miles (60 km) each day. If necessary, the animal can go without a drink for four to seven days.

Your job isn't finished once you've reached your destination — a port on the Mediterranean or a town on the edge of the desert. Unlike in today's business deals, the South Arabian merchant who hired you as caravaneer didn't agree on a price for his goods before shipping them to his customer. In this kind of long-distance "venturing," the merchant depends on your skills as a salesman to arrive at a good price with buyers.

IF YOU CAN'T RAISE CROPS, RAISE CAMELS

Pastoralists are people who live in dry areas where it is difficult to grow crops. Instead, they raise animals. In the Iron Age, camel pastoralists in Arabia drank the milk of camels, spun their wool, made their skin into containers, carved their bones into tent pegs, used their dung for fuel, and ate their meat on special occasions. They traded extra male camels from their herds to caravaneers for food and other items that didn't exist in their desert habitat.

Spice Merchant

Caravan Stop Owner

No one ever seems satisfied with what they can grow in their own backyard. Your customers could make do with homegrown spices — cumin, coriander, dill, thyme, and mint — but they prefer the exotic spices you've bought from an Arab caravaneer. They use them for special skin creams and medicines as well as for flavoring food.

Your donkey carries your goods as you walk to each of the bazaars, or marketplaces, in your region. Iron Age roads go around cities, rather than through them, because the cities so often sit on hills and are enclosed by walls. You have to turn aside from the main road onto the path to each settlement. The one-lane roads to the cities are unpaved, and rivers must be forded (crossed on foot). Fortunately, your donkey's ancestors have been beasts of burden since 4000 BCE, so he's not likely to trip or to let you down.

Once you reach the bazaar at a city's gate, you get down to business. The cost of your spice? It doesn't have a sticker price. You haggle with your customer. "But this cinnamon comes all the way from India," you might say, arguing back and forth until you arrive at a mutually agreed-upon amount.

You run a donkey caravan stop on the Way by the Sea, a road that runs north from Egypt along the eastern shore of the Mediterranean through the Philistine lands. Your customers depend on you to provide pasture land for their donkeys, access to water, an area to camp, and fresh food supplies. You may also raise donkeys for the caravan trade and collect customs charges for the king.

Resin Tapper

Perfumer

When we cut ourselves, a scab forms on our skin. When a terebinth, or turpentine, tree is cut, a yellowy, strong-smelling substance called resin oozes out of its bark. "Tapping" a tree for its resin sounds a little tame for what you do. In the spring, you hack the tree with an ax to get the resin flowing. All summer long, you visit your trees in the mornings, after the cool night air has thickened the resin. You scrape the precious resin off the trunk and from the flat stones you've placed at the bottom of each tree.

Why is terebinth resin precious? It is used in incense (a substance burned in religious ceremonies), perfumed body oils, and healing ointments. Since each tree produces only small amounts, and trees can't be tapped every year, resin is expensive.

How "nosy" are you? A perfumer must have a sensitive nose. In an age in which people wash their hands and feet but seldom take a bath, everyone's counting on your skill. Both men and women wear your perfume on their clothes or skin to hide body odor.

The ingredients in your perfumes are expensive, because most of them are imported from other lands. You stir flowers, plants, or fragrant wood into olive oil, leave the mixture for a time, and then press or squeeze out the perfume from the softened petals and sticks. Because your perfumes are oil-based rather than alcohol-based like today's perfumes, they protect the skin from drying out on hot days and keep it sweet-smelling — to other people. A bonus is that flies and mosquitoes hate its strong scent.

Salt Maker

People around the world have always craved salt. It not only makes food tastier but also preserves it. In the Bible Lands, people pickle everything from figs and olives to fish and grasshoppers in brine — a mixture of salt and water.

Unlike imported spices, salt won't make you a rich man. If something is scarce, it is expensive, but salt can be found throughout the region. Since you live beside the Mediterranean, you produce salt for local use by boiling sea water in a pottery vessel over a fire. It's a simple job, but very important. One of today's scholars ranks preserving food with salt right up there with the tanning of hides and the making of metal as one of the human race's most important achievements.

THE VERY SALTY SEA

Ancient travelers from Jerusalem bumped along over a rough track that fell 4,000 feet (1219 m) across 20 miles (32 km) to the Dead Sea, the lowest place on earth. It is also one of the saltiest. The sea is one-third solid, its shores crusty with salt. The salt collectors working along its coast who went for a dip must have been as surprised as later visitors at the water's buoyancy. "It was a funny bath. We could not sink ... and came out coated with salt till we shone like icicles," wrote American author Mark Twain.

CHAPTER 9

AT-SEA JOBS

Sailing on the Mediterranean must have been thrilling, like train travel in the mid-nineteenth century or air travel in the early twentieth century. Although it was expensive to build ships and hire sailors, travel on land was slow. Moving large quantities of goods, particularly metals, by water was easier than moving them on the backs of donkeys or in carts. Everything from the ordinary (olive oil and wood) to the exotic (monkeys and ostrich eggs) found its way onto a ship.

The Phoenicians impressed their neighbors with their seafaring skills. Phoenicians were also ahead of their time in finding markets for their crafts far from their own land. They even imported other people's wine and olive oil and then rebottled it for export to distant ports.

Pirate

Like pirates today, you count on surprise and a well-armed crew to overpower trading ships. So that you can sneak up on your prey, you've had the sails and ropes of your ship dyed the color of the sea. The roundish merchant ships sailing on the Mediterranean in the sixth century BCE are no match for your sleek galley powered by oars and sail. If you catch a tub with its sail rolled up in a strong wind, you can attack it and board before its captain has a chance to set sail and get away. You and your crew also raid villages along the coast, plundering them for cattle, goods you can trade elsewhere, and people to enslave.

What's another name for you? Water rat.

"O strangers, who are you? From where have you come along the sea lanes? Are you traveling for trade, or are you just roaming about like pirates?"
— Homer, *The Odyssey*, an epic poem from ancient Greece

Fisher

During the fishing season, you and your father and brothers head out onto the Mediterranean in two small boats. Once you're in deep water, you fling a large net between the boats. Both teams then slowly paddle back to shore side by side, dragging the seine net behind and with it the catch of the day — sea perch, sea bream, and mackerel. Fishers on inland lakes and rivers use hooks and lines, spears, and small nets.

Since fish spoils quickly, coastal fishers probably smoke, dry, or salt part of their catch for sale to landlocked towns and cities.

WHY IS THAT HORSE SWIMMING OUT TO SEA?

The Phoenicians carved horse heads on the bows of the small boats they used for fishing, carrying sandstone blocks from coastal quarries, and transporting goods short distances. Some scholars think the carvings may have represented a mythical winged seahorse, which the ancient Greeks called the *hippokamp*. In artwork from the time, a sea god is sometimes shown riding on the back of this strange creature. The Phoenicians may have believed that the horse-head prow, because of its connection to a marine god, would protect a boat and its crew from danger.

Shipbuilder

Business people who "run a tight ship" are strict managers. You probably run a tight ship, too, but you also build one. Like those of the mason, your building materials fit very closely together. His stone walls stand firm with no mortar gluing them together. Your warship's lightweight hull stays waterproof without the help of gucky caulking smeared between the planks.

Your secret? A plan drawn up by a master shipbuilder, good measuring skills, and expert carpentry. To fit two planks together, you and your carpenters first chisel out several slots (mortises) in the side of each plank. You insert small pieces of wood (tenons) into the mortises of the first plank. Wooden pegs (dowels) hold the tenons in place. (Today some prefabricated furniture is put together at home with dowels.) Then you fit the second plank's mortises over the protruding tenons on the first plank and hammer its dowels into place with your mallet. Repeat, plank after plank after plank, until you have a hull.

When the boat is launched, the water will swell the wood, making the ship watertight. For 2,000 years, Mediterranean shipbuilders used mortise-and-tenon carpentry to build most of their ships.

"They that go down to the sea in ships, that do business in great waters; These see the works of the Lord, and his wonders in the deep."
— Psalms 107:23

Sailmaker

At the beginning of the Iron Age, you are busy making a new type of sail, one that can be drawn up, or furled, like a modern window blind. You weave your sail fabric from thread spun from the parts of the flax plant that carry water. This makes a sail that doesn't rot and fall apart in stormy seas. After you have woven many squares of linen, you and your helpers sew the pieces together, making a giant patch-work sail.

Or do you? That's what the sails look like in some ancient drawings, but divers on the Mediterranean shipwrecks from your era have come up empty-handed. Archeologists don't know much about you or your work, because not even a tiny piece of your square linen sails has survived. Your sails are waterproof, but not that waterproof.

Anchor Maker

"Stop the boat!" the captain cries. You make it possible for the ship's crew to carry out his order. Sailors depend on your anchors to moor their ships at sea, particularly when "evil winds" threaten to sweep them onto a reef or rocky cliff. The wooden and iron anchors of later centuries have two arms in a V for gripping the sea floor. Your squarish anchors carved from stone blocks depend on their weight (from 120–200 pounds/265–440 kg) to hold the ship in place.

In addition to the main rope hole you've drilled near the top of the anchor, don't forget to chip out an L-shaped hole in a lower corner. If the heavy anchor gets stuck between rocks on the bottom, sailors can free it by yanking on a second rope looped through this hole.

Porter

Loading a Phoenician ship requires good balance and strong fingers. In the warehouse near the harbor, you pick up two amphorae (pottery jars) filled with wine, olive oil, or food by looping a few fingers of each hand through the jars' handles. You carry the jars down to the ship, up the narrow gangplank, and into the hold. You and your fellow porters do this over and over again, until the ship's hold contains up to 350 amphorae, all tied together by a rope threaded through their handles.

If you helped load the eighth-century BCE ship called the *Tanit*, all your work was for nothing. The amphorae, filled with wine, sank with the ship and weren't discovered until 2,700 years later, scattered on the muddy bottom of the Mediterranean.

THE TIN CANS OF THE ANCIENTS

The amphora was the Iron Age's tin can. People in the Bible Lands used this fat, carrot-shaped pottery jar for thousands of years to ship olive oil, wine, incense, and honey. Its pointy bottom made it possible for hundreds of amphorae to be nested together in a ship's hold. Since these jars were all about the same size (4 gallons/18 liters), archeologists believe they may have been mass-produced in large pottery workshops. Traders reused amphorae until they broke.

Mole Builder

Oarsman

This job builds good "abs" and tones arm and leg muscles. But unless you enjoy vigorous rowing, that's about the only good thing that can be said about it. You and your 14-foot-long (4 m) oar are not much more than one leg of a seagoing centipede. Along with your fellow oarsmen, you stand up on each stroke, then pull back on your oar as you fall back on your bench.

Your steady rowing is equal to about 1/10 of a horsepower. Even when all of you are rowing as hard as you can, your ship moves slowly by today's standards, at less than 9 miles (15 km) an hour. However, if your commander can steer your ship close enough to the enemy's, that's enough speed to slice off the other boat's oars in a sneak attack — as long as you and the other oarsmen pull in your own oars at the last minute.

Obviously, you don't make furry little animals with long noses. The other meaning for mole is "breakwater." And "breaking water" is exactly what you hope to do with your offshore stone wall. Moles are built to make an artificial harbor or to protect the entrance of a natural harbor from stormy seas or attack. They also provide a quay where ships can dock.

Your mortarless wall will be built on a sandstone reef or a low rocky island. First, you and your crew must make the reef or island level, to provide a good foundation for the 50-foot-wide (15 m) mole. Then you begin laying rows of large, carefully cut blocks with their "headers," or ends, facing the oncoming waves. The friction of the long sides of each block against the adjoining ones helps the breakwater stand up to the destructive force of the sea.

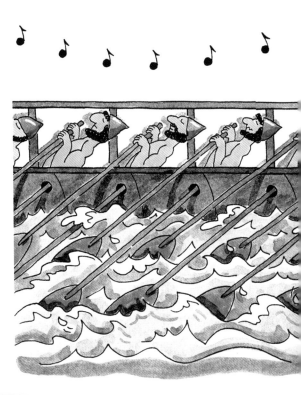

Pipe Player

TOOT, toot, TOOT, toot. If you can play a few notes over and over again on a recorder, why not apply for this job? On a warship, you set the pace for the oarsmen with your clay or reed double-pipe. Try not to have a fit of sneezing in the middle of a battle, though, or the crew will lose their rhythm and the captain will yell at you — or worse. SPLASH!

Navy Commander

Before the eighth century BCE, military commanders used ships to transport troops or as platforms for archers and lancers fighting battles at sea. The ship you command, however, is a true fighting machine, equipped with a new weapon — a pointed battering ram used to rip open a hole below the waterline of an enemy ship.

You might think this is a straightforward job — point and bash — but it isn't. First, the ram needs rowing power behind it to penetrate the enemy's hull. You must man your double-decker *bireme* with as many as 36 strong oarsmen in two rows on each side. Second, you must select and train your crew well. At your command, they must be able to change direction quickly, maneuvering your ship into position for attack. Finally, after ramming the stern or side of the enemy vessel, your crew must quickly row backwards to open the wound and swamp the other ship.

STRIKE NOW, MEN!

Cargo Ship's Pilot

Probably you would rather be working on a fast-moving warship than on a Phoenician *gôlah*, a wide "tub" built for carrying large loads long distances. But don't worry — even if you're a speed demon, you won't be bored. Finding your way to and from Mediterranean ports without compasses or navigational instruments of any kind takes great skill.

Sailing by sight only is called piloting. Storms and fog prevent merchant and navy ships from sailing during the winter, but the rest of the year you navigate by looking for familiar landmarks. Wherever you are on the Mediterranean, you can usually spot a mountain on the mainland or on an island in the distance. If you climb up the mast, you can see about 6 miles (10 km) farther than you can from the deck. If you are still unable to sight land, you can release one of the crows or doves carried onboard. Since these birds can't land on the water, they will soar into the air, then make a beeline for the nearest shore.

At night you steer by the stars, particularly the pole star in the Ursa Major (Great Bear) constellation. It was the Phoenicians who discovered that navigators could use this bright star to steer in a north–south direction.

Go find the shore, dovey.

CHAPTER 10

RELIGIOUS JOBS

It's all very well to be "sticky" people — to stick together and to stick around when the going gets tough. But like all ancient peoples, those in the Bible Lands also relied on the help and protection of gods and goddesses in their daily lives. They believed the gods controlled the power of nature and its cycles of life and death.

The Canaanites, and later the Phoenicians, worshiped several gods, with El being the most powerful. He was married to Astarte, the goddess of love and war. Other major gods included Baal, the god of storms and rain; Yam, the god of the sea; Eshmun, the god of healing; and Mot, the god of the underworld and death. According to one myth, Mot overcame Baal during the dry summer months, but Baal returned with the fall rains. The Philistines had similar gods and goddesses.

People worshiped at private shrines in their homes, at raised altars built outside, and in public temples. (Phoenician sailors, for example, visited special seaside temples before setting out on a voyage.) They burned incense and sacrificed animals as gifts to the gods. As in all agricultural societies, people held religious festivals to celebrate seasonal events, such as harvests and sheep shearing.

In Israel some people began worshiping one god, Yahweh, as the divine king and father of the people. Three later religions — Judaism, Christianity, and Islam — are rooted in this ancient religion. All three still set aside one day a week for rest and worship, as did the ancient Israelites on the Sabbath.

High Priest

"Powerful" is a good word to describe you. In Phoenicia, you are the second most important man after the king. This explains why priests are the best-dressed people in Phoenician society, aside from the royal family. Your fine linen robes are embroidered with colored linen thread and interwoven with thin gold wires.

You are in charge of the main temple in your city, which is protected by its own special god and goddess. The temple has a courtyard with a large altar where you perform animal sacrifices on behalf of your people. The congregation worships inside the temple, and you offer special prayers in a small room called a sanctum. In times of plague, drought, and other disasters, when the gods are angry, you are particularly busy praying and performing special rites. In addition to priests and possibly priestesses, your temple employs musicians, servants, and even barbers to shave the priests' heads.

Like all priests in the Bible Lands, you are respected as a wise man, a judge, and a teacher and guardian of the sacred traditions of your people.

Levitical Priest

Your job is hereditary — it is said that your ancestors can be traced to the tribe of Levi. All of the men of your Israelite family work as religious specialists. In the temple, you assist the high priest and other priests (*kohen*), who are descended from the priestly clan of Aaron. They are the only priests who can ask for and deliver Yahweh's blessing to the people. As a Levitical priest, you organize the music for the services, make sure that the temple and its altars are cleaned, and help prepare the animal sacrifices and offerings of oil, wine, and bread.

Temple Musician

The priests have blown their long silver or bronze bugles to call the people to the temple for worship. After everyone has gathered, you follow the singers and drummers in the procession into the inner sanctum. You play a lyre — a wooden instrument with four to eight strings that you pluck like a harp.

After the Babylonians forced the Israelites into exile and destroyed the temple in Jerusalem, the Israelites created new religious rituals. On their return to Jerusalem in 538 BCE, only men were allowed in the temple's inner sanctum. Your job disappeared.

Prophet

What was your role in Israelite society? And were there prophetesses, too? No one in the present day knows for sure. Some scholars believe Yahweh communicated with the people through prophets like you. Others think your job was to express hope for the future. You may be a member of the royal court and serve as an adviser to the king. Or you may be a reformer from the lower classes who speaks out against injustice and oppression.

Translations of the Hebrew word for "prophet" include "one who speaks in the name of a god" or "an interpreter of the will of a god," but these are guesses at best. Most scholars who study the Bible agree that you were a public speaker, so if you're shy, this won't be the job for you.

Necromancer

Your fancy job title simply means that you communicate with the dead. Actually, there's nothing simple about that, is there? In fact, it sounds a bit spooky. During the Iron Age, though, the spirits of ancestors were thought to be very powerful. You consult the dead on behalf of their relatives. You ask the spirits not only to give advice, but also to use their special powers to bring good fortune to their families.

How do you talk with ghosts? Ancient texts from Mesopotamia say you tweet like a bird, because the dead were believed to look and sound like birds.

Guardian of the Field

Professional Mourner

You used to be a clan elder, and people in your village looked up to you. Now they are afraid of you. Your new job is to guard a large fallow field. Farmers allow fields to rest every seventh year, so that the soil can replace the natural minerals crops remove from it. However, farmers working in faraway fields need someone to guard their fallow fields from sneaky neighbors who might try to sow a crop on them. As a dead ancestor, you make the perfect watchman. No one would dare rob your family of their land with you buried in the field. Yes, that is the one drawback to this job: you must be dead to apply.

If you feel sad for your friends when they are upset, or the tears start to flow when you watch sappy movies, this may be the job for you. Fortunately, it's part-time.

When a family member dies, the family hires you and other professional women mourners to cry and sing sad songs at the funeral. Your weeping, called keening, is seen as a sign of respect for the dead person. Like other people attending the funeral, you wear clothing made of sackcloth (a rough woven material), and cover yourself in ashes. It may seem like a depressing job, but you know you are bringing comfort to the family as you honor their loved one.

CHAPTER 11

MILITARY JOBS

Warriors armed with slings and arrows in ancient pictures don't look very dangerous. Looking at them, you might think, "War couldn't have been so bad back then." But war in the Bible Lands was every bit as destructive then as it is now. The Iron Age saw the rise of large, organized armies with professional commanders, spies, and scribes who kept track of the names of those called up for military service. The battles in this era involved more men than at any time until the American Civil War. Whole cities were destroyed, and victorious armies carried off the "spoils of war" — cattle, horses, camels, goods, even people.

Charioteer

Armorer's Assistant

You and your fellow charioteers form the strike force of the Canaanite army. In 1200 BCE, each city-state's king depends on his elite corps of chariot warriors to defend his territory. You and your driver, along with other two-men teams, patrol the rocky plains around the city. You protect trade caravans, ambush enemy patrols, and team up with "chariot runners" (spearmen on foot) to attack invaders on the battlefield.

The wooden chariot serves as a platform for well-trained archers like you. Be prepared for a bumpy, exciting ride — your chariot has no springs, and the wheels are made of wood.

You'd better be a "knotty" girl in this job. Chariot drivers and archers can't carry shields, and they can't hope to duck all the arrows on the battleground. A helmet and the 12-pound (5 kg) suit of body armor your family makes protect them.

Your job is to tie hundreds of 3-inch-long (8 cm) metal scales in overlapping rows onto the armor's leather tunic. You thread a skinny leather strip through the pairs of holes in the scales and the matching holes in the tunic and tie a knot. (It's a little like sewing a button onto a shirt.) Tie your knots tightly. A charioteer could die if his scales fall off in battle, leaving bare spots for the enemy's arrows to find their mark.

Commander of the Army

By the time of King David (1005–961 BCE), the Israelites have added better-trained militia, professional soldiers, and mercenaries (paid combat soldiers from other lands) to their army. As its commander, you no longer have to worry about battles on the open plains or large numbers of militiamen deserting. Before the king made you commander-in-chief, you proved yourself a brave warrior by leading your clan's "thousand" (*'elep*), the largest unit in the militia. In peacetime, you make sure the army is well fed, trained, and housed. In times of war, you are second in command to the king.

Light Infantryman

Although you are a farmer, not a foot soldier, the leader of your clan has ordered you to serve in the Israelite militia, a non-professional people's army. You are worried about how your family will get along without you, but you have no choice. Once a clansman turns 20, he must serve in times of war.

Before you leave your village, you pack some food (raisins and dried figs are good choices, since they last a long time) and arm yourself with a sling or spear. You also tuck a dagger, a short sword, into your belt. You don't own armor or a helmet. They are expensive and, in any case, would weigh you down during the swift, surprise attacks on the enemy in Canaan's hilly countryside.

Heavy Infantryman

As a Philistine foot soldier, you belong to one of the first professional armies to be equipped with iron weapons. You must be strong to fight with your heavy 3-foot-long (1 m) iron sword in one hand and your iron-rimmed wooden shield in the other. Years of training by officers of your city's warrior class have prepared you for battle. Before an attack, you put on your leather body armor and strap on your helmet. The helmet's wraparound crest, possibly made of reeds or stiff leather strips, helps you identify your fellow soldiers quickly in combat. It also adds height and, along with your bulky armor, makes you look more terrifying to the enemy.

Hand-to-hand combat between two champion warriors of opposing armies was once used by your people as a way to settle battles. The famous biblical story of David of Israel and the Philistine Goliath of Gath describes this type of warfare. In the story, the giant Goliath challenges the Israelites to send out a soldier to fight him. Only David is brave enough to step forward. He kills the Philistine not with a sword, but with his simple sling and some stones.

"They shall run like mighty men; they shall climb the wall like men of war; and they shall march every one on his ways, and they shall not break their ranks."
— Joel 2:7, comparing locusts to soldiers attacking a city

Groom

You feel very lucky to be working and living in the most modern royal horse stables of ninth-century Israel. King Ahab's architect designed the new stables for the city of Megiddo, creating several buildings with stalls for about 450 chariot horses. As one of the grooms, you brush the horses assigned to you, "muck out" their stalls (your least favorite chore), and lead your horses out to the pasture. You also drive a cart pulled by a donkey up and down the center aisle of your stable, stopping at each stall to shovel hay and grain into the feeding troughs. More than 2,500 years later, the teeth marks of your horses will still be visible on these limestone mangers set between the pillars of the stables.

Victory Drummer

Would you like to be a drummer in an all-girl band? Although more men than women play drums today, the opposite seems to have been true in ancient Israel. You play a frame drum (*tof*) made of animal skin stretched over the two sides of a wooden hoop or frame. Holding the drum in one hand, you bang it with the other. You accompany the other women in your group as you sing and dance to welcome soldiers home after their victory in battle.

UNDER SIEGE

Some historians believe that by the beginning of the Iron Age, siege warfare was already 5,000 years old. The Assyrians perfected this terrifying type of assault. As well as attacking a city gate with their battering rams, they built sloping earthen ramps wide enough for several rams up to the city wall. The defenders' archers tried to set the wooden rams on fire with flaming arrows, while the attackers tried to start fires inside the walls with their own "messengers of death."

HOW FAR, HOW FAST?

• In three minutes, a good archer could shoot thirty arrows, a rate that firearms wouldn't achieve until the late nineteenth century CE.
• In five days, 9,500 men could build a siege ramp to the top of a 70-foot-high (21 m) city wall.
• With his slingshot, a slinger could hurl a stone the size of a tennis ball 300 yards (274 m).

Sapper

Zing. Zing. ZING. That was close! What's it like to be the main target of the enemy's archers? Become a sapper and you'll find out.

During a siege, rather than climbing a ladder and going over the city wall, sappers tunnel under or through it. The enemy is desperate to prevent you from opening a way into their city. Their best archers stand on top of the wall and fire arrows straight down on you. Others drop stones. Only your tall shield of woven reeds protects you. Since you can't defend yourself, you hope your own army's archers will provide enough covering fire to allow you to do your time-consuming work.

Using pickaxes and pry bars, you and the other Assyrian sappers open a large hole in the stone wall. You prop up the wall with wooden posts as you dig. When the hole is deep enough, you set fire to the supports, collapsing the wall in that spot.

Battering Ram Engineer

Like today's tank engineer, you are in charge of designing and building an armored combat vehicle. In fact, the tank traces its roots back to the ancient battering ram. To modern eyes, your four-wheeled *kar* might look like an over-sized wooden toy, but it was the most deadly war machine known in the seventh century BCE. Unlike a tank, your siege engine is pre-fabricated — the Assyrian army can transport it in pieces to their destination and put it together on the spot. It will be used to bash down the gates or walls of a city your ruler wants to conquer.

CAMEL WARRIORS

The Bible and Assyrian records from the ninth and eighth centuries BCE both mention Arab camel warriors. The warriors rode in pairs, one guiding the camel and the other firing arrows while seated on the dromedary's hump. When Samsi, an Arab queen who controlled trade routes in northern Arabia, lost a war with the Assyrian king, Tiglath-Pileser III, he rounded up thousands of her camels as plunder.

Cavalryman

The horses of antiquity were small — the size of today's ponies. Don't let their size fool you into thinking this job is a ride in the park, though. During battles, you will be galloping bareback over rough ground — in ninth-century Assyria, saddles and stirrups hadn't been invented yet.

You and another cavalryman ride as a team. You hold a shield and the reins of both stallions while your partner shoots arrows at the enemy. Your work requires courage, strong muscles, good teamwork, and excellent horsemanship. No wonder the writers of the Old Testament called you "hurricanes on horseback."

Now That's Insulting!

"You're a cooking fire that goes out in the cold ... a waterskin that soaks the one who lifts it, limestone that crumbles in the stone wall, a battering ram that shatters in the land of the enemy, a shoe that bites the owner's foot."
— *The Epic of Gilgamesh*, from Nineveh, Assyria, seventh century BCE

"The elements necessary for man's life are water and fire and iron and salt and wheat flour and milk and honey, the blood of grapes, olive oil and clothing."
— Ecclesiasticus, a Hebrew book of wisdom from the second century BCE

The Troubled Times Continue

"**T**oday is not the end. Today we bury our dead, and we pick ourselves up," said a Palestinian teenager in 2009 after yet another war had ended. "Picking ourselves up" after wars continues to be a sad fact of life in the Bible Lands.

Following the Iron Age, the little land bridge at the end of the Mediterranean remained under the control of various empires. Whether people were ruled by the Roman and Byzantine empires of the Christians or the Islamic Turkish empire, cities came under siege, bridge dwellers revolted against the laws of their new masters, wars were won, and battles were lost. People moved into the region (Arabs from the east) or away from it — the descendants of the ancient Israelites founded Jewish communities around the world.

After the founding of the Jewish state of Israel at the end of the Second World War, a series of wars broke out between the new country and neighboring Arab states. Civil war in Lebanon added to the unrest in the region, which continues today. Yet the people of these lands still farm and look for ways to cope with scarce water supplies. They still make practical tools and beautiful artwork; they still flock to markets and sing and dance at festivals. While they wait for politicians to find peaceful solutions to the problems of the Bible Lands, the inhabitants of the region find strength and hope, as they always have, in their families, friendships, religious faith, work, and play.

Recommended Further Reading

Broida, Marian. *Ancient Israelites and Their Neighbors: An Activity Guide* (2003).
  This book is a fun way to learn about the ancient Israelites, Philistines, and Phoenicians. It has 35 hands-on projects that you can do, from making blackberry dye to constructing a model Phoenician trading ship.

Dig magazine, the archeology magazine for kids, has a website, www.digonsite.com, for those of you interested in digging up the past.

Robb, Don. *Ox, House, Stick: The History of Our Alphabet* (2007).
  An interesting look at how the alphabet created in ancient times in the Bible Lands changed over many years to become the alphabet we use today.

Tubb, Jonathan N. *Bible Lands* (2000).
  Hundreds of photographs of fascinating artifacts illustrate this Eyewitness Book tracing the early history of the region.

Williams, Marcia. *God and His Creations: Tales from the Old Testament* (2004).
  Well-known Bible stories, including Noah's Ark, David and Goliath, and Daniel in the Lion's Den, are retold and illustrated in comic-strip style.

For those of you in Grade 6 and up:

Panchyk, Richard. *Archaeology for Kids: Uncovering the Mysteries of Our Past* (2001).
  The 25 projects in this book, from pottery classification to making an oil lamp, help readers learn about the techniques used by archeologists in their work.

Ellis, Deborah. *Three Wishes: Palestinian and Israeli Children Speak* (2004).
  Young people from Israel and the Palestinian territories describe their daily lives, their fears, and their hopes for the future.

Acknowledgments

The work of many authors has made this book possible. In particular, I would like to acknowledge the work of Philip J. King and Lawrence E. Stager. A special thank you to Tim Harrison for his advice. Any errors are mine alone. My thanks to editor Barbara Pulling, designer Sheryl Shapiro, illustrator Martha Newbigging and the team at Annick Press for their outstanding work. I would also like to acknowledge the support of the Ontario Arts Council.

Index

Ahab, king of Israel, 88
alloys, 52
alphabet, 10–11
amphorae, 75
ancestors, 16, 82
anchor maker, 74
animal sacrifices, 80, 81
animal trainer, 21
apprentices, 31, 55, 58, 59
Arabia, 55, 67, 90
Arabian desert, 66, 67
Arabs, 67, 90, 92
archeologists, 11, 12, 13, 26,
    27, 42, 43, 49, 55, 57, 58,
    61, 74
archer, 59, 77, 85, 89, 91
armor, 85, 86, 87
armorer's assistant, 85
army, 33, 84, 86, 87, 90
arrowhead maker, 52
Ashkelon, 11, 13
ashlar blocks, 46
Assyria, 8, 15, 91
Assyrians, 49, 56, 89, 90
Astarte, 79
awl, 46, 64
ax, 45, 46, 52

Baal, 79
Babylonia, 8, 15
Babylonians, 81
baker, 41, 50
bandits, 67
barber, 80
Barclay, Dr. James Turner, 49
barley, 19, 24, 27, 41
baskets, 26, 48, 62
baths, 69
battering ram, 77, 89, 90
    engineer, 90
bazaar (market), 17, 37, 40,
    68
beam-press, 42
beds, 29
Be'er Sheva, 38
beetle carver, 57
Bible, 10, 12, 22, 31, 40, 52,
    55, 67, 73, 82, 87, 91
Bible Lands, 10, 12, 13, 14,
    15, 18, 92

social structure, 16–17
    timeline, 14–15
birds, 21, 25, 40, 78
bireme, 77
boats, 72
bodyguard, king's chief, 31
bow drill, 46
bow maker, 59
bowyer, 59
boys, 17, 21
bread, 27
    maker, 27
    ovens, 27, 41
breakwater, 76
brick(s), 44, 47
    maker, 44
bronze, 50, 52
    arrowhead maker, 52
Bronze Age, 52, 57
brooch, 62
building materials, 22, 43, 44,
    45, 46, 47, 73
bulla, 32
bull-roarers, 17
burial, 13, 58
butcher, 40
Byblos, 45

calendar, 19
calves, 21, 63
camel(s), 66, 67, 90
    warrior, 90
Canaan, 6–8, 14, 57, 58
Canaan dog, 26
Canaanites, 6–8, 10, 57, 79, 85
caravan, 66, 67, 85
    stop owner, 68
caravaneer, 67, 68
cargo ship's pilot, 78
carpenter, 46, 56, 73
Carthage, 14, 42
casemate wall, 38
cavalryman, 91
caves, 58
cedar, 30, 45
cemeteries, 48
charcoal maker, 51
charioteer, 85
chariots, 85, 88
cheese, 34

chickens, 40
children, 11, 13, 17, 20, 28,
    58, 65
chisel, 31, 46, 48, 52, 56, 73
Christianity, 79
cisterns, 28, 47
cities, 14, 16, 17, 37, 40, 44,
    68, 80, 84, 89, 90
    royal, 17, 38, 39
city-state, 14, 29, 85
clamshells, 57
clans, 16, 18, 23, 81, 83, 86
clay, 44, 53, 58, 59, 61
    coffin maker, 59
clerk, 11, 42
    inventory, 33
climate, 7, 28, 39, 47
cloaks, 60, 62
cloth maker, 55, 61, 74
clothing, 55, 60, 62, 80, 83
coffin maker, 59
comb maker, 64
commander of the army, 86
composite bow, 59
cook, 35, 50
cooking, 13, 20, 35
copper, 48, 50, 52
coprolites, 13
corvée official, provincial, 36
cosmetics, 42, 57, 65, 68
court scribe, 30
craftspeople, 16, 54–59, 63
Crete, 57
crop(s), 9, 13, 16, 18, 19, 21,
    24, 67, 83
cubit, 44
cuneiform writing, 10
Cyprus, 57
Cyrus II, king of Persia, 15

dancing, 88
date(s), 26
    picker, 26
David, king of Israel, 14, 29,
    31, 45, 86, 87
Dead Sea, 46, 70
deer, 40, 59
desert, 66, 67
detergent, 61
diet, 24, 25, 27, 35, 40

disease, 18, 20
doctor, 20
dogs, 13, 23, 26, 39, 49
donkeys, 18, 24, 28, 39, 67,
    68, 88
drinks, 35, 41
dromedary, 67, 90
drought, 8
drummer, 81, 88
dry season, 7, 28
dung, 23, 39, 63, 67
    fuel maker, 27
dye, 62
    factory owner, 62

earthquakes, 46
Ecclesiasticus, 91
Egypt, 7, 8, 14, 42, 45, 55, 57, 68
Egyptian(s), 53, 56, 59, 64, 65
    hieroglyphs, 10
    pharaohs, 7, 45
Ekron, 42
El, 79
elder, 16
    city, 37
    village, 19, 83
elephants, 51, 56, 57
Elissa, 42
engineer
    battering ram, 90
    planning, 44
Epic of Gilgamesh, The, 91
Eshmun, 79
excrement, 13, 27
eye makeup mixer, 65

fallow fields, 83
families, 16, 18, 19, 29
famine, 8
farmer, 16, 17, 18, 19, 21, 24,
    83, 86
farming, 7, 9, 16, 18–19,
    21–26
feast days, 23, 24, 35, 40
fibula maker, 62
figs, 70, 86
firewood, 47, 50, 51, 58
fish, 36, 70, 72
fisher, 72
flatbread, 27

Look for these other great books in Annick's JOBS IN HISTORY series ...

"Witty, charming, and packed with information."
—*VOYA*

Archers, Alchemists, and 98 Other Medieval Jobs You Might Have Loved or Loathed

Cowboys and Coffin Makers
One Hundred 19th-Century Jobs You Might Have Feared or Fancied

"Undeniably captivating ... Highly Recommended."
—*CM Magazine*

Ballplayers and Bonesetters
One Hundred Ancient Aztec and Maya Jobs You Might Have Adored or Abhorred

"A great way to learn about an ancient civilization."
—*City Parent*

Pharaohs and Foot Soldiers
One Hundred Ancient Egyptian Jobs You Might Have Desired or Dreaded

"... a clever approach to teaching kids about ancient Egyptian life."
—*School Library Journal*